My Sacred Bull - 4

AF624745

Insights from

Love and Logic

In Arrangement with *Financial Chronicle*

My Sacred Bull - 4

Insights from Love and Logic

In Arrangement with *Financial Chronicle*

Kuruvilla Pandikattu SJ
Professor of Physics, Philosophy and Religion
Jnana-Deepa Vidyapeeth, Pune

CWI

Christian World Imprints(TM)

© Financial Chronicle

Kuruvilla Pandikattu SJ asserts the moral right to be identified as the author of this book.

First Published in 2017 by

Christian World Imprints™
Christian Publishing & Books from India
H-12 Bali Nagar, **New Delhi-110015**
info@christianworldimprints.com
www.ChristianWorldImprints.com
Phone: +91 11 25465925

ISBN-13: 978-93-5148-167-6 ISBN-10: 93-5148-167-0

Cataloging in Publication Data--DK
Courtesy: D.K. Agencies (P) Ltd. <docinfo@dkagencies.com>

Pandikattu, Kuruvila, author.
Insights from love and logic : in arrangement with Financial chronicle / Kuruvilla Pandikattu SJ.
pages cm. -- (My sacred bull ; 4)
Includes bibliographical references.
ISBN 9351481670
ISBN 9789351481676

1. Spiritual life--Christianity. I. Title. II. Series: My sacred bull ; 4.

BV4501.3.P36 2016 DDC 248.4 23

All rights are reserved. No part of this publication can be reproduced, distributed, performed, publicly displayed, stored in a retrieval system, made into a derivative work, transmitted or utilized in any form or by any means; electronic, mechanical, photocopying, recording or any information storage system, without the prior written permission of the copyright holder(s), as indicated, and the publishers.

Jurisdiction: Any conflict or dispute in relation to this publication shall be adjudged in accordance with the laws of India and the matter shall be subject to the jurisdiction of the Courts, Tribunals or any other Forums of New Delhi, India, only.

Disclaimer: The views and contents of this publication are solely of the Author(s); the Publisher may not subscribe to them.

Printed in India.

Dedicated to:

Those who taught me that the logic of love is
paradoxically different from the logic of reason;
that genuine love always involves immense suffering;
that there is true joy in genuine love and
concomitant suffering;
that love is everything.

The Book

What is the relationship between love and logic in actual life? What is the relevance of spirituality for the contemporary men and women who do not have the luxury to spend hours in prayer? Can spirituality emerge from the ordinary, boring and mundane experiences of an average human being? Open-minded and visionary, the articles in this book are meant to touch the daily life of busy people who are fully involved in the struggles and success of daily life. Limited to 625 words, they appeared first in the *Financial Chronicle,* one of the most prestigious business and financial newspapers of India, and they attempt to provide us with both roots and wings: rooted that will give them a sense of belonging to the rich Indian heritage and wings that will take them forward based on the spiritual depth. This book, *Insights from Love and Logic: In Arrangement with Financial Chronicle* is a humble attempt to lead genuine spiritual life in our contemporary context.

The Author

Professor Kuruvilla Pandikattu SJ holds two doctorates and has been involved in creative dialogue between science and religion. Author/ editor of more than 40 books, he teaches philosophy at Jnana-Deepa Vidypeeth: Pontifical Institute of Philosophy and Religion and is a regular columnist for *Financial Chronicle*, Hyderabad. He is a Jesuit priest belonging to Dumka-Raiganj Province and an accomplished teacher and writer in making religion relevant to our times. He may be contacted at kuru@kuru.in. See sites: www.kuru.in and www.jdv.edu.in

Foreword

More than ten years ago, *Financial Chronicle*, India's first global business networking platform, was looking for spiritually focused, knowledge-driven content to inspire and enrich its educated audience of business leaders, managers and corporate executives. Editor-in-chief Shubhrangshu Roy, who conceived the daily newspaper and initiated the project "My Sacred Bull," on the editorial page of *Financial Chronicle (FC)*, asked me to discover an enlightened thinker to address the existential yearnings of intelligent India and FC's wider global audience.

I turned to Professor Kuruvilla Pandikattu SJ for his innate wisdom. He is a priest, physicist and philosopher, adorned with three masters' degrees and two doctorates. His creative spirit and open vision had long inspired me. The professor-priest readily obliged, taking pen to paper week after week to script a volume that has now acquired epic proportions. His insightful column is deeply relished and respected by FC's global band of dedicated readers.

Prof Pandikattu's articles stand out for three characteristics that uncommon in both spiritual and scientific discourses:

Contextual sensitivity: Normally he takes up a current event – from politics, science or religion – and reflects on it giving it a spiritual basis and contemporary relevance.

Religious openness: Committed to his Catholic faith, his critical and creative acceptance of other religious and non-religious traditions is extraordinary. Without falling into eclecticism, he has a way of drawing the positive aspect of every experience.

Forward movement: His writings pursue our quest as individuals and communities, to move ahead in our pilgrimage of life, conquering new peaks. He is convinced that the Spirit is working within us to move us to another level, where human beings can live in peace and harmony, affirming and respecting the differences that exist among each other.

By and large, these spiritual essays are non-denominational and are not limited to any religious group. At the same time, they open the inquisitive spirit in us and thus widen our experience. As such, his columns are very inspiring and forward-looking.

I am happy to note that he has handpicked the best of the articles that he has scripted for FC and is publishing them in this book: My Sacred Bull-IV: *Insights from Love and Logic in arrangement with Financial Chronicle*. As of today more than 400 well-appreciated articles of Prof Pandikattu have appeared in our "My Sacred Bull" column, which has been appearing in the "My Mind" section of *Financial Chronicle* for six years now. Truly a great achievement! I recommend this book whole-heartedly for its inquisitiveness, spiritual depth and universal openness.

Dr. Michael Gonsalves
Senior Assistant Editor
Financial Chronicle

Acknowledgements

In bringing out this book, I am immensely grateful to Mr. Shubhrangshu Roy, the Chief Operating Editor and Editor-in-chief, *Financial Chronicle (FC)*, who has requested me to write these articles.

I am also indebted to Mr. Michael Gonsalves, Senior Assistant Editor, *Financial Chronicle*, who has designed the column "The Sacred Bull" and has been constantly urging me to contribute my share to it.

With a deep sense of gratitude, I want to acknowledge the role played by the staff and students of Papal Seminary, Pune and Jnana-Deepa Vidyapeeth, Pune, India, for providing me with the facilities and opportunities for these insights.

Finally, I am indeed grateful to the Almighty, who makes all things happen, so that we may "live, move and have our being" in Him, who is our Everything.

Kuruvilla Pandikattu SJ

Contents

Introduction

The logic of love is very different from that of the practical organised life. So, Blaise Pascal could claim that "heart has its own reasons, which reason does not know of." Or Shakespeare says poetically: '"Love looks not with the eyes, but with the mind,/ And therefore is winged Cupid painted blind." This book, the fourth volume in the series of Sacred Bull, is a collection of articles on life, love and spirituality for common people.

All of them were especially written for *Financial Chronicle* (FC), from the Hyderabad-based Deccan Chronicle Holdings Ltd, which was launched on 16 April, 2008, by India's youngest team of media professionals, and in the shortest-ever run-up for a newspaper.

As such the articles are meant for a general audience, who may or may not be organisationally religious. They are meant to inspire a band of young men and women to think deeply about themselves, leading to deeper insights and wisdom.

Open-minded and visionary, these articles are meant to touch the daily life of busy people who are fully involved in the struggle and success of daily life. So, the articles are limited to 625 words. And these articles attempt to provide them with both roots and wings: roots that will give them a sense of belonging to the rich Indian heritage and wings that will take them forward based on the spiritual depth.

Though the author gladly acknowledges his Christian commitment, he does not impose it on the audience. Trying to be objective and philosophical, as much as possible, the articles are an open invitation to search for deeper meaning and widen vision.

For clarity and convenience, these articles are roughly divided into eight approximate and arbitrary sections.

i. Religion and Life
ii. Stories that Connect
iii. Poetry and Language
iv. Spirituality and Service
v. Science and Religion
v. Depth of Life
vii. Keys to Happiness
viii. Suffering and Evil

The presupposition of these articles is that spiritual life has to be based on day to day experiences of ordinary people and so God has to be found in our daily life. When we reflect on daily events, we can truly be open to the deepest mystery, that guides us forward. A cautious and courageous attitude is necessary in this search. Truly optimistic and open-ended, these articles urge the readers to find the depth of existence in the ordinary things of the world and thus make the sacred emerge from the mundane. In that sense, even though some of us refuse to believe in God, as a species, we can claim to be a special and unique species: in fact the only one who can and needs to make such a claim!

Religion and Life

1

Religion too Needs Innovation, Change

Nidhal Guessoum, astrophysicist and associate dean at the American University of Sharjah, tries to convince his fellow citizens to take modern science seriously, with all its methodology, results and limits. But he finds the reverse-exercise, to try and convince scientists and other educated people that religion should be taken seriously, much more difficult.

"Religion relates to an organised system of beliefs (theology), practices (rules and rituals) and relations at both individual and communal levels (church, community, society, etc.). In his article, "Why Should Scientists Care About Religion?" Guessoum urges discerning people "not to confine their ideas to such simplistic and cartoonish views of religion, forgetting that religions, western and eastern, have developed rather advanced and sophisticated theologies" (Guessoum 2013).

He pleads for refined, and 'cultivated' religion, which can present very attractive, 'updated' theologies. One of the first criteria, or even litmus tests, for such 'updated' theologies is "their degree of compatibility with modern science, a sine qua non condition." He asks scientists to take seriously such "advanced, open-minded, open-ended and 'updated' theology or religion," since it addresses a dimension of human life that can rarely be illuminated by science.

Normally 'believers' claim that their religion brings to them the following: a personal purpose and meaning to one's life, a perspective on things, a sense of identity, an emphasis on love as the most important factor in life, a communal bonding and support, moral guidance and compass, and a greater ability to cope with death and disasters. Further, believing scientists add 'a unified worldview', whereby the universe 'makes more sense'. Guessoum acknowledges that the feelings of awe, wonder and mystery that believers feel are also shared by 'spiritual atheists'. However, believers also find in religion "a harmonious explanation for all of existence, with its physical and metaphysical dimensions, mental, spiritual, relational and communal. And it unifies the ideas of life and death."

Many religious people, academicians and scientists hold that their beliefs help them deal with the question of what it means to be human. Again, due to a large spectrum of beliefs that people hold, "what it means to be human" can range from "being in the image of god" to 'having a spirit' or even just 'a higher level of consciousness'. In any case, one can see that such personal beliefs, whether constructed for oneself or taken from the teachings of one's religion, can be genuinely humanising. Guessoum hopes that science, with its limitations, must be accepted and upheld by all, believers and non-believers, particularly by educated persons. He acknowledges that faith, spirituality and religion are "optional sets of ideas that one may choose to carry or not, in one version or another." However, educated and discerning people, in particular, must strive to make faith, spirituality and religion as sophisticated, open and updated as possible.

Religion needs to pose direct questions to today's human beings and offer relevant answers to contemporary concerns. So, religions need to update themselves, just like sciences.

Just like innovation and change are necessary parts of science, religion also needs to accept change, innovation and adapt itself to the needs of our present world. Religion needs to pose direct questions to today's human beings and offer relevant answers to contemporary concerns. So, religions need to update themselves, just like sciences. When such updated religion encounters science, both are enriched and humanness is fostered. Such critical and creative encounters help humanity.

2

Religion Must not be Linked to Superstition

A prominent campaigner against religious superstition has been shot and killed in the city of Pune. Narendra Dabholkar, aged 67, was at the forefront of a long-running campaign to ban superstitious religious practices by getting the state of Maharashtra to pass an anti black-magic bill. He died on August 20, after being shot by gunmen riding a motorcycle.

Dabholkar had infuriated some extremist Hindus with his campaign to outlaw the religious practices of some ascetics. Many 'godmen' have claimed to perform miracles so as to impress their devotees. They claim to "summon spirits, conjure up objects, provide talismans for curing ailments, walk on fire and pierce their tongues with steel skewers" (Rahman 2013).

Dabholkar's anti-superstition organisation, the Maharashtra Blind Faith Eradication Committee, had offered a reward of Rs 5 lakh to anyone claiming to be a spiritual diviner, who could successfully summon spirits. "What has happened is shocking. It is really shameful," said Vijaya Chauhan, a close friend and associate of Dabholkar. "The best way to pay homage to a man who had been campaigning relentlessly for the past 18 years for a law against superstitious religious practices is to immediately pass the bill in the state legislative assembly."

Some politicians in the state strongly opposed the bill and even the ruling Congress party seemed to lack the political will to push ahead with the legislation, though the bill was passed immediately after his assassination. Besides lobbying in the legislature, Dabholkar's group was involved in a school outreach programme across Maharashtra, which encouraged rational thought among students and exposed religious charlatans. Dabholkar was qualified as a doctor but gave up his profession to devote himself to the rationalist cause. He edited a weekly magazine and was closely associated with the founder of the Indian Rationalist Association, Sanal Edamaruku, who fled to Europe following death threats and blasphemy cases against him (Rahman 2013).

It is unfortunate that a country like India, which has always tolerated or even accepted heterodoxy, cannot accept rationalism or atheism. Religious persons' primary duty is not to impose their religion on others, but to be faithful to their own religious commitment. Unfortunately, like most other human enterprises, religion can also become corrupt catering to the interests of the greedy and the privileged. Under such circumstances, rationalism and atheism may serve the purpose of purifying religion.

Whoever has killed Dabholkar has not done religion any service. On the other hand, a murder committed in the name of religion is all the more atrocious, since religion is primarily meant to foster brotherhood and common life. A religion that becomes a weapon of the evil forces is both diabolically dangerous and self-destructive. We need to protect ourselves from such religious fanaticism, more than from rational criticism. Superstitions and violence are more detrimental to religion than searching, criticising and questioning. Any religion that cannot accept criticism from its own rank and outsiders is a disservice to humanity.

> Sometimes God is much more pleased with genuine atheists than with violent and selfish theists.

Many eminent religious leaders themselves — including Socrates, Jesus and Buddha — have been accused of atheism. It is perfectly all right for a believer to practice one's religion, but not to use violence on another. If God can allow different religions, including rationalism and atheism, to flourish, who are we to deny the right of existence to atheists and non-believers? Sometimes God is much more pleased with genuine atheists than with violent and selfish theists.

3

Personal Religious Conversion is Vital

How does religion transform us? Why should there be continuous personal conversion? Facing personal religious conversion is no easy task. Perhaps, one can speak about a double edge. One is sharp and the other, soft, said professor Chae Young Kim, president, Korean Academy of Religions and professor of religious studies at Sogang University, South Korea. He referred to two prominent religious thinkers, William James, an American psychologist and Bernard Lonergan, a Canadian theologian, to illustrate his point.

Lonergan develops his theory of conversion within his wider philosophical context. His concern with the human subject as the locus of authenticity in all human activities is something that can be expanded and applied to other fields and disciplines. In attending to Lonergan's philosophy of conversion, we can "think about its broad implications and about how this philosophy can impart a new orientation to the study of conversion as a human phenomenon," says Kim.

Kim relates Lonergan's philosophical study of religious conversion to the psychological study of religious conversion as this is occurring in a number of modern academic disciplines (Lonergan 1992). Before Lonergan took up the study of conversion as key for human understanding, many North American classical thinkers already had an interest in pursuing this issue as a compelling topic of interest in their academic works. The academic study of religious conversion as a key focus of interest in the psychology of religion first arose and developed in the 19th century. At that time, this was seen as a uniquely intellectual theme of interest which gained broader acceptance only in the 20th century.

One prominent school that arose at Harvard University in the wake and under the influence of William James's study was of religious experience. Especially after giving the Gifford Lectures in Edinburgh in 1900, his psychological study of religious experience was so well received that many students and scholars pursued this subject. This school became known simply as the Harvard school (James 1936). It focused more qualitatively on the importance of biographical and phenomenological research on personal conversions and, as a result, the research was not limited to the kind that can come from rigorously engaging in experimental psychology.

Kim thinks that this approach should be retrieved in order to work beyond a social scientific study toward a more comprehensive understanding of religious conversion by revisiting James's thought and attending to how it relates to Lonergan's work. Above all, Lonergan's comprehensive study of conversion can be related to James' earlier broad study of conversion. James also examined wide ranges of human phenomena and tried to identify the interior source of all human phenomena in terms of conversion. Thus, James's study of conversion was not simply limited to religious dimensions but all conversions of human life.

In the process of ongoing religious conversion, James and Lonergan placed a different accent on religious emotion. James thought of religious emotion as combining the joyful and the fearful. He emphasised these two aspects equally and named it as the "solemn emotion." We need to remind ourselves that being a religious person implies

> We need to remind ourselves that being a religious person implies experiencing ongoing personal conversion and transformation. A scientific and interdisciplinary study of conversion — religious, ideological and cultural — can basically enrich our understanding of human beings.

experiencing ongoing personal conversion and transformation. A scientific and interdisciplinary study of conversion — religious, ideological and cultural — can basically enrich our understanding of human beings.

4

Can Religion Foster Good Behaviour?

What would the world be like with no religion? While this is a question we shall probably never answer fully, we can always explore this question further. Does religion contribute, on balance, to human well-being or to oppression and misery? The article titled "Would the World Be Better Off Without Religion? A Skeptic's Guide to the Debate," offers us a new perspective. What is significant is that the place it is published — *The Skeptical Inquirer*. It is probably the world's best-known atheistic periodical for challenging unscientific or pseudoscientific claims and "isn't exactly a platform for pro-religious cheerleading." The two authors of the article, Scott O. Lilienfeld and Rachel Ammirati, are researchers at Emory University and self-confessed atheists (Lilienfeld&Ammirati. 2014).

This makes Lilienfeld's and Ammirati's conclusions — couched as they are in the cool, almost irritatingly self-distancing language of professional sceptics — all the more remarkable. They certainly don't make religion look like the *summum bonum* of all human affairs. But they are very certain that it is not the opposite, either. According to the wide-ranging literature they survey, there is a regular but modest positive correlation between religiosity and prosocial behaviour, and a negative correlation between religious practice and antisocial behaviour. These correlations persist across a wide range of study designs and methods, suggesting a genuine correlation.

> "Belief in God bears a statistically significant, albeit relatively weak, association with lower levels of criminal and antisocial behaviour, including physical aggression toward others."

Lilienfeld and Ammirati were inspired to carry out their investigation by the self-assurance and vociferousness with which people on both sides of the debate typically broadcast their claims. Writers such as Richard Dawkins, Sam Harris, and Daniel Dennett confidently proclaim that there are few or no social benefits of religion, despite devoting virtually no space in their books to objective examination of the research. Meanwhile, pro-religion voices, such as author Rick Henderson, boldly state that atheism leads to immorality, despite extensive demographic and research evidence to the contrary.

The researchers dived deep into the growing body of quantitative studies, meta-analyses, and experimental evidence to determine whether religion was a net negative for humanity. They operationalised "goodness" as prosocial behaviour, in the assumption that when writers claim we'd be "better off" with or without religion, they're implicitly referring to a more humane world in which people treat each other more kindly, says Connor Wood, a researcher at Boston College, writing in *Patheos.*

Surveying dozens of published research studies tackling exactly this question, the sceptics found that a consistent effect emerged: across studies, religious believers were slightly less likely to do antisocial things than their completely secular counterparts. The authors hold that "recent studies, as well as meta-analyses of the literature, have converged on a consistent conclusion: belief in God bears a statistically significant, albeit relatively weak, association with lower levels of criminal and antisocial behaviour, including physical aggression toward others." Thus, Lilienfeld and Ammirati propose a well-argued case that religion is not the anathema many anti-religion activists make it out to be. However, this doesn't mean that atheists are automatically immoral (Lilienfeld & Ammirati. 2014).

The two authors, as sceptics attempting to grasp the truth of anti-religious and pro-religious claims, are admirably circumspect in their conclusions. "The evidence is clear that at the individual level religion is weakly associated with prosocial behaviour."

5

Between the Plausible and the Ridiculous

Many people come to their religious commitments slowly, carefully and deliberatively, as if the attitude they take toward life itself depends upon their judgment. Many struggle, at one point or another, in a pluralistic, science-sophisticated society, with the despair that it all might be a sham. Most people, whatever their religious persuasion, assume there are decent human beings with good intentions who interpreted the evidence differently and who are wrong.

If faith is a conjecture or a leap into the unknown, as Sören Kierkegaard said, perhaps understanding what is ridiculous and impossible makes people feel safer about where that leap might land them. Renée Haynes, a writer and member of the prestigious British Society for Psychical Research introduced the concept of the "boggle threshold": "the level above which the mind boggles when faced with some new fact or report or idea." Each of us have these boggle lines, regarding our own faith, claims T M Luhrmann, a professor of anthropology at Stanford University writing in *The New York Times* (Luhrmann 2014).

The boggle lines tell us something about our belief and non-belief. Each of us has what we could call a belief continuum, "with taken-for-granted obvious truths at one end and whacked-out possibilities at the other." When we draw a line between the plausible and the ridiculous — our boggle line — we become more confident about the beliefs on the plausible side of the line. You are, the boggle line tells you, a sensible, reasonable person. You do not believe in that. So a belief in the opposite can be seriously considered.

Benoit Monin, a professor of organisational behaviour and psychology at Stanford and his colleagues have found that when people do something that affirms their lack of prejudice, like disagreeing with blatant racism or expressing willingness, in a laboratory experiment, to hire a black person instead of a white one, that reasonable moral action seems to licence them later to express views that seem racist. Seeing yourself as morally reasonable might allow you to make morally risky choices (Luhrmann 2014).

So, perhaps, rejecting the extreme position might make a less extreme, but still uncertain, commitment seem more plausible. We can make a case that this is why heresy is so important in every religion. "What people do not believe is often more clearly articulated than what they do believe," the sociologist Lester R Kurtz wrote, "and it is through battles with heresies and heretics that orthodoxy is most sharply delineated." The sociologists would explain if this is true, it is because people unite most profoundly in opposition to a common enemy, says Luhrmann.

> In the face of our own uncertainty, being precise about what we don't believe in (ridiculous) can shore up the confidence in what we do (plausible). Thus, our faith and commitment are moves between the ridiculous and the plausible.

Faith asks people to consider that the evidence of our senses may be partly wrong. In various ways, and in varying degrees, faith asks that "people believe that their minds are not always private; that persons are not always visible; that unseen presences should alter your emotions and direct your behavior; that reality is good and justice triumphant." These are fantastic claims, and the fact of their improbability is not lost on those who accept them, adds Luhrmann. Gods are invisible, the future is inscrutable. God is unknowable. We see through a glass darkly. The long tradition of spiritual literature is full of intense uncertainty about god's true nature. In the face of our own uncertainty, being precise about what we don't believe in (ridiculous) can shore up the confidence in what we do (plausible). Thus, our faith and commitment are moves between the ridiculous and the plausible.

6

Developing Moral, Spiritual Capacity

Writing in *The Huffington Post*, Noam Chomsky, Professor Emeritus, MIT department of linguistics and philosophy asks the basic question: "How many minutes to midnight?" (Chomsky 2014). Given the atomic arsenal at our disposal, he was asking how long we can prevent total destruction.

According to Chomsky, if some extraterrestrial species were compiling a history of *Homo sapiens*, they might well break their calendar into two eras: BNW (before nuclear weapons) and NWE (the nuclear weapons era). The latter, of course, opened on August 6, 1945, the first day of the countdown to what may be "the inglorious end of this strange species," the only one to have attained "the intelligence to discover the effective means to destroy itself," but, "not the moral and intellectual capacity to control its worst instincts."

Day one of the NWE was marked by the "success" of the Little Boy, an atomic bomb. On day four, Nagasaki experienced the technological triumph of Fat Man, a more sophisticated design. Five days later came what the official Air Force history calls the "grand finale," a 1,000-plane raid attacking Japanese cities and killing thousands of people, with leaflets falling among the bombs reading "Japan has surrendered."

Those were the auspicious opening days of the NWE. As we now enter its 70th year, Chomsky wonders how we have survived till now. He questions how many more years can we survive the danger of nuclear calamity. Chomsky quotes General Lee Butler, former head of the US Strategic Command, which controls nuclear weapons and strategy. Twenty years ago, he wrote that we had so far survived the NWE "by some combination of skill, luck, and divine intervention, and I suspect the latter in greatest proportion" (Chomsky 2014).

Reflecting on his long career in developing nuclear weapons strategies and organising the forces to implement them efficiently, General Butler described himself ruefully as having been "among the most avid of these keepers of the faith in nuclear weapons." But apologetically, he came to realise that it was now his "burden to declare with all of the conviction I can muster that in my judgment they served us extremely ill."

The general poses the question: "By what authority do succeeding generations of leaders in the nuclear-weapons states usurp the power to dictate the odds of continued life on our planet?" He observes that it is a "near miracle" that we have escaped destruction so far, and the longer we tempt fate, the less likely it is that we can hope for divine intervention to perpetuate the miracle. Butler's sober assessment should be a wake-up call for all of us.

> Unless we draw from them and experience our own best potentials, we are helplessly leaving our destiny merely to our "skill, luck and divine intervention."

Chomsky refers to our "moral and intellectual capacity" to control our worst instincts. Together with them, we may also add our spiritual capacity and resource to control ourselves and our worst fears (Chomsky 2014).

Confronted with the exponential technological advancement, together with its dangers and fears, we need to develop our moral, intellectual and spiritual capacity to encounter the worst — fears, risks and dangers — so that we can experience the best in ourselves. In spite of the doom around us, we still have deep and collective spiritual resources and wisdom experienced and elaborated by our poets, mystics and sages. Unless we draw from them and experience our own best potentials, we are helplessly leaving our destiny merely to our "skill, luck and divine intervention." Synergistically, we need to draw the best in our hearts to marvel at ourselves and the cosmos.

Stories that Connect

7

Reading Stories Can Alter How We Think

A recent study has shown that reading stories actually changes our brain. Scholars at Emory University, Atlanta, US, have detected actual changes in the brain that linger for a few days, after reading a story.

"Stories shape our lives, and in some cases, help define a person," asserts neuroscientist Gregory Berns, lead author of the study and the director of Emory's Centre for Neuropolicy. "We want to understand how stories get into your brain, and what they do to it" (Emory Health Sciences 2014). Research using functional magnetic resonance imaging (fMRI) has begun to identify brain networks associated with reading stories. Earlier studies have focused "on the cognitive processes involved in short stories," forgetting the subjects actually reading them, claim the authors.

The study focused on the lingering neural effects of reading a narrative. 21 undergraduates participated in the experiment, which was conducted over 19 consecutive days. The study was published in journal Brain Connectivity and reported in *DailyScience*. All of the study subjects read the same novel, Pompeii, a 2003 thriller by Robert Harris based on the real-life eruption of Mount Vesuvius in Italy. "The story follows a protagonist, who is outside the city of Pompeii and notices steam and strange things happening around the volcano," Berns says. "He tries to get back to Pompeii in time to save the woman he loves. Meanwhile, the volcano continues to bubble and nobody in the city recognises the signs." The researchers chose this exciting book because "it depicts true events in a fictional and dramatic way" (Emory Health Sciences 2014).

For the first five days, the participants came in each morning for a base-line fMRI scan of their brains in a resting state. Then they were given nine sections of the novel, about 30 pages each, over a nine-day period. After reading the assigned portion in the evening, they took a quiz in the morning to ensure that they actually read it. Then the participants underwent an fMRI scan of their brain in a non-reading, resting state. After completing the whole novel, the participants returned for five more mornings to undergo additional scans in a resting state.

"Your favourite novels could certainly have a bigger and longer-lasting effect on the biology of your brain."

The results showed heightened connectivity in the left temporal cortex, an area of the brain associated with receptivity for language, on mornings following the reading assignments. "Even though the participants were not actually reading the novel while they were in the scanner, they retained this heightened connectivity," Berns claims. "We call that a 'shadow activity,' almost like a muscle memory." Heightened connectivity was also seen in the central part of the brain. "The neural changes that we found associated with physical sensation and movement systems suggest that reading a novel can transport you into the body of the protagonist," Berns says. "We already knew that good stories can put you in someone else's shoes in a figurative sense. Now we're seeing that something may also be happening biologically" (Emory Health Sciences 2014).

The neural changes persisted the morning after the readings, and for the five days after the participants completed the novel. Bern asserts that "the fact that we're detecting them over a few days for a randomly assigned novel suggests that your favourite novels could certainly have a bigger and longer-lasting effect on the biology of your brain." If reading a story can actually change the brain, praying or meditation can also do. Even believing in God may change our brain. Thus, our religious faith and stories may alter our brain structure. These are areas needing further experimental research.

8

Connect Your Life Story to Spirituality

In his new and insightful book *Spirituality and Your Life Story*, Bradley Hanson, emeritus professor of religion, Luther College, US, probes the close connections between spirituality and one's personal "life story" (Hanson 2014). Each of us has come to our present life stance through a journey of unique experiences — being born at this time, growing up in this particular social setting and culture, experiencing these specific successes and losses, and having these significant relationships. Whether we are in the early, middle, or latter part of our personal faith story, the ending is still ahead of us — and reviewing our own faith story helps us chart our course into the future.

Hanson uses ground-breaking insights of Dan McAdams, professor of psychology at Northwestern University, that in our teen years, people begin to form their personal identity by projecting what they might do and become. He says that people imagine a narrative of their life and as events occur, they modify their "life story" and fashion it in dialogue with story lines in their surroundings.

Based on empirical evidence, McAdams advances a three-level concept of personal identity in which the various elements of the self are integrated through composing and revising our own life story. He proposes an interview structure to plot the story line of a person, which he used extensively for his research. To discover the story of each new person he met, Hanson started with the simple question: "Tell me about yourself" (Hanson 2014). The answer he received though usually dealt only with surface facts, which could be the starting point to discover the complex and larger story of the concerned individual.

McAdams has devised a series of questions that helped Hanson draw out much of the inner narrative of people. Questions about key life events proved most fruitful: a peak experience, a low experience, a turning point, and questions about an important event in childhood, adolescence and adulthood. He used a modified version of this life story interview and related it to the spiritual aspirations of various people.

This personal experience and discovery have led Hanson to probe the interconnections of this book's three major themes — spirituality, personal identity and life story.

Hanson's main insight is that "we make sense of life by composing our own life story." After opening with an account of the life story understanding of personal identity, spirituality and one's own life story, Hanson considers our major story lines: childhood family, success, romantic love, friendship, revenge-apology-forgiveness and loss. Then he considers the "master stories" of scientific atheism and theism that address our most fundamental human questions ('Spirituality and Your Life Story' 2014).

Thus, the book explores how our personal identity and spirituality are influenced by the values embedded in our childhood family life and major story lines promoted by our culture. Combining personal interviews, spiritual reflection, and psychological research, Hanson considers our most basic quest to make sense of life.

Such personal identity and spirituality is concrete and contains genuine stories of success, love, friendship, forgiveness and loss. In our search for spiritual wholeness and fulfilment, we cannot forget the concrete person with her individual experiences, yearnings and dreams. A spirituality that provides us with a meaningful personal identity and draws a personal story within the larger story of the cosmos can enhance us.

"We make sense of life by composing our own life story."

9

How We Can Connect Ourselves to Others

Most of us have difficulty in being true to ourselves or being authentic with others. The foundation for healthy and vibrant connections is forged through authentic mutual sharing of what each person is experiencing inside, along with how they communicate their experience to each other.

Being authentic with oneself points "toward an ongoing process of uncovering what's percolating deep inside us," writes John Amodeo, author of *Dancing with Fire: A Mindful Way to Loving Relationships* (Amodeo 2013).

According to Amodeo, writing in "World of Psychology," authenticity "involves a sincere effort to go inside ourselves and uncover what we're actually experiencing, and then communicate that. True authenticity requires that we pause and check in with ourselves before responding, rather than sloppily venting emotions in a reactive way." Amodeo suggests two key ingredients that foster interpersonal and authentic engagement. The first is being mindful. There can be no authenticity without mindful awareness of what we're actually experiencing. Mindfulness for Amodeo is "attending to our experience just as it is without judging ourselves."

Oftentimes, we don't allow ourselves to experience what is because it is contaminated by shame. We imagine that something is wrong with us for having particular feelings. We try to fit ourselves into some image of how we think we need to be in order to be respected or loved. We judge ourselves as weak or defective if we experience sadness, hurt, or fear. We may be convinced that if we showed vulnerability to others, they would reject us.

But vulnerable feelings are simply a part of being human, Amodeo reminds us. "It's a great strength to embrace our humanity, not a weakness. Bringing a gentle mindfulness to the full range of our human experience and disclosing this to people we want to be close to create a climate for rich connections" (Amodeo 2013). Such a mindfulness connects us to ourselves and others. It creates a foundation for being more intimate with others. By allowing a person to see what's real for us, we invite them into our heart.

The second ingredient is being kind. All of us know people who are kind but emotionally dishonest. They hide their genuine feelings, leaving us to guess about how they feel or what they want. It's difficult to connect with people who are not sincere and direct. We may choke on their sweetness when it's not linked with authenticity. On the other hand, "mindfulness wedded to kind communication is a powerful force. Being aware of our feelings and wants and conveying them in a kind way is more likely to be well-received."

"It's a great strength to embrace our humanity, not a weakness. Bringing a gentle mindfulness to the full range of our human experience and disclosing this to people we want to be close to create a climate for rich connections."

Human hearts are tender. People become less defensive and more receptive when we communicate our feelings, not only genuinely, but with a gentleness that shows how vulnerable we ourselves are.

So Amodeo says, "I notice how connections become deeper and sweeter as the couple becomes mindful of what they're authentically experiencing — and as they cultivate the courage and skills to convey this in kind and gentle ways." He adds, "Rather than struggle to change, fix, or analyse each other, love thrives in a climate of mutual authenticity bathed in the gentle waters of kindness. People who feel safe being together are drawn into a deeper participation in each other's hearts" (Amodeo 2013).

Can we be mindful and kind, so that we can reveal ourselves truly and authentically? Such authentic sharing of our dreams, wishes and disappointments bring us closer to the other, who are as broken and vulnerable as we are. That leads to a loving and spiritual relationship.

10

Why Are Choices Important to Life?

Our memory is extremely personal, while at the same time, supremely collective. We all have our own particular catalogue of recollections. But we are all also part of a greater story, and our lives intersect with each other in such complex and dangerous ways that the shared memory of what we have been to each other shape how we live with each other. That is, in short, the history that humans possess, says A G Harmon, writing in *Patheos* (Harmon 2014).

Harmon's writing refers to American writer Lois Lowry's classic young adult novel, *The Giver* (Lowry 2014). It has been brought to the screen on August 15, 2014. In the movie, memory is not allowed to the individual members of the state. Memory is the repository of only one who retains the past in case it's ever needed. As he ages, he must give his storehouse to another.

The reason for this state of affairs is that in hopes of ridding the world of misery, the society has decided simply to stop remembering it altogether. That can only be accomplished by stopping all that would bring misery to the world. The implication is that the world as we know it consists of highs and lows, peaks and valleys, heavens and hells. As such, it is a world of chance — one in which we have the power to make paradise or perdition. That is what the world is. In defiance of that fact in *The Giver*, the choice has been made to end all choice. The argument implies that when the individual is left to his own devices —ignorant, greedy, lustful, lazy, wrath-prone wretch that he is — he will most often choose wrongly. Better to parcel out what he really needs — what he isn't smart enough to know he does.

This will necessarily require a certain amount of surrender from the part of the people. To end agony by eliminating memory, you must also end ecstasy. "The human condition is such that the possibility of the good is dependent upon the risk of the bad; the dimensions of life only rise into fullness when all things are potentialities," claims Lowry.

The assumption is that misery, which we dread, is a consequence of the "conflict over differences." If all is equal, down will go sickness, crime, poverty and loneliness. But it also implies that individuality must go, as well as initiative and competition — because they only cause conflict. And you have to take away risk and profit because such possibilities allow for loss and devastation. So the best way to stop envy is not to have success; the most thorough means to end sadness is by way of ending its opposite, joy. One is not sad if there is no concept of bliss, writes Harmon (Harmon 2014).

Now, these things can only be experienced in particular manifestations of the lived world — through music, poetry, art, love-making, friendship, family. Consequently, these realities must be modified, clipped or trimmed so that they actualise the good of all. Further, not everyone can enjoy what is actualised. In a finite world, only so much can go around. So, the unfit, the surplus, must give way to those deemed worthy. So, it is truly ironic, that the age-old drive for egalitarianism ends in the persecution of the truly low — those who "drain" resources.

We need to recognise that in spite of the limitations, we have to respect the choice others make, both responsible and irresponsible. For freedom is basic to human dignity.

Of course, words lose meaning when there is no contrast. If we eliminate degrees, we begin to lose the concepts of heat and cold, and finally, through disuse, the ability to distinguish them. We need to recognise that in spite of the limitations, we have to respect the choice others make, both responsible and irresponsible. For freedom is basic to human dignity.

11

When Profit Takes Over Public Interest

How have we transformed ourselves as a community? Professor Neal Postman was one of the few who sensed the tremendous transformation that is taking place in us. His book *Amusing Ourselves to Death* (1985) was a perceptive and prophetic warning to each one of us.

He persuasively argues that news and information were becoming entertainment, that the media — especially the electronic media — are overwhelming us with undigested information.

One of the hallmarks of a free and democratic nation is the importance of informed citizens. The citizens need to understand the danger of state-operated information services, and need to get accurate and unbiased information on the public's business. Such is the importance of the freedom of the press.

As Gary Hart, the American politician, writes in his "Matters of Principle" blog, says that Professor Postman was a pioneer in pointing out that "the trivialisation of genuine news into entertainment" (Postman 1985). It began with the sensationalism by the tabloid media. Later on it went on to "demonise" traditional liberalism and its adherents, "to ridicule traditional media" or the so called 'lamestream media'. Instead of trying to provide accurate reporting, tabloids fixated on "scandals," becoming "the messy process of democracy itself" (Hart 2012).

Scandal begets scandal. Hart argues that "despite high-minded rhetoric about informing the people, the tabloid revolution has provided more entertainment and distracting 'amusement' than unbiased and authentic coverage of important public matters." He bemoans the fact that "during the finest days of print journalism, many, if not most, newspapers were owned by public-spirited local families who put the interests of their communities ahead of profit." When profits began to fall, the business people took over those papers and the television and radio stations. They began "to sacrifice the public interest for profit." The emergence of entertainment industry replaced accurate reporting and objective analysis with fanciful entertainment programmes (Hart 2012).

When reporting the news in a balanced and informative way does not bring profit, it is understandable the media was shifting toward the more profitable entertainment industry. Therefore, we meet plenty of youngsters who can give the names of all the movies produced in a year, but not the number of states in India. We have many people who are well-versed in the achievements of the sportspeople, but not in the basic tenets of the faith of her friend's religion.

The greater the public ignorance, the less effective the government, the less vibrant our democracy and less genuine our spiritual search. For those who despise democratic government and promote clashes between groups, keeping the people ignorant becomes imperative.

> "Despite high-minded rhetoric about informing the people, the tabloid revolution has provided more entertainment and distracting 'amusement' than unbiased and authentic coverage of important public matters."

Today's political, philosophical and religious leaders need to realise that gradually we are becoming a society addicted to entertainment and thus "amusing ourselves to death." If we are not well-informed we cannot make balanced decisions for the collective good of our nation.

Thus, it is of extreme importance that we need to be truly informed, that we choose and discern. We cannot bury ourselves in superficial data. Obviously, we need entertainment and relaxation, but it has to be intertwined with life. The critical and creative dimension of entertainment and art have to be rediscovered. Without them our political and religious future is at stake!

"Despite high-minded rhetoric about informing the people, the tabloid revolution has provided more entertainment and distracting 'amusement' than unbiased and authentic coverage of important public matters."

12

How Storytelling Can Connect Us Internally

We all enjoy a good story, whether it's a novel, a movie or simply something one of our friends is explaining to us. Why are we so engaged when we hear a good narrative about events or persons?

It's, in fact, quite simple. If we listen to a discussion or a powerpoint presentation, a certain part in the brain gets activated. Scientists call this Broca's area and Wernicke's area. Overall, it hits our language processing parts in the brain, where we decode words into meaning.

On the other hand, when we are being told a story, things change dramatically. Not only are the language processing parts in our brain activated, but "any other area in our brain that we would use when experiencing the events of the story are too," writes Australian author Leo Widrich in *LifeHacker*, a weblog site (Widrich 2012).

If someone tells us about how delicious certain foods were, our sensory cortex lights up. If it's about motion, our motor cortex gets active. Metaphors like "The singer had a velvet voice" and "He had leathery hands" activates the sensory cortex. A story can put our whole brain to work. When we tell stories to others that have really helped us shape our thinking and way of life, we can have the same effect on them too. The brains of the person telling a story and listening to it can synchronise, confirms Uri Hasson, a researcher from Princeton University.

In an experiment, when the woman narrated her story, the volunteers understood her story and their brains synchronised. When she had activity in her insula, an emotional brain region, the listeners also had it. When her frontal cortex lit up, so did theirs. By simply telling a story, "the woman could plant ideas, thoughts and emotions into the listeners' brains."

Using the power of a story, we can get others also experience anything that we experienced ourselves. When the narrator and the listener have the same brain areas activated, they feel really connected. A story, if broken down into the simplest form, is a connection of cause and effect, writes Widrich. And that is exactly how we think. We think in narratives, no matter if it is about buying groceries, our job or our success. We make up short stories in our heads for every action and conversation. That is simply because our brain is wired to listen to stories or perceive cause and effect. That is why, Jeremy Hsu, a researcher from Stanford University, found that "personal stories and gossip make up 65 per cent of our conversations" (Widrich 2012).

Whenever we hear a story, we want to relate it to one of our existing experiences. That's why metaphors work so well with us. While we are busy searching for a similar experience in our brains, we activate the insula area in the brain, which helps us relate to that same experience of pain, joy or disgust. This happens to most people: a good friend tells us a story and then two weeks later, we mention the same story to him, as if it was our idea! This is totally normal. It shows that this is one of the most powerful ways to get people on board with your ideas and thoughts. According to Uri Hasson, "a story is the only way to activate parts in the brain so that a listener turns the story into their own idea and experience." Hasson sums it up, "Storytelling is the only way to plant ideas into other people's minds" (Widrich 2012).

> "A story is the only way to activate parts in the brain so that a listener turns the story into their own idea and experience."

We need to realise that as human beings, we are all part of the larger story of the universe and of living beings. Our spiritual quest is part of the interconnected and shared story that makes our lives significant.

13

Gaining Wisdom through Stories

We live in a world awash with information, but we seem to face a growing scarcity of wisdom. What's worse, we confuse the two. We believe that having access to more information produces more knowledge, which results in more wisdom. But, if anything, the opposite is true, writes the famous Bulgarian thinker Maria Popova in *Brain Pickings* (Popova 2014).

This barrage of readily available information has also created an environment where one of the worst social sins is to appear uninformed. Ours is a culture where it is really embarrassing not to have an opinion on something. In order to seem informed, we form our so-called opinions hastily, based on fragmentary bits of information and superficial impressions rather than true understanding.

The American poet Ralph Waldo Emerson holds: "Knowledge is the knowing that we cannot know." To grasp this insight, we first need to understand knowledge as a ladder of understanding.

At its base is a piece of information, which simply tells us some basic fact about the world. Above that is knowledge — the understanding of how different bits of information fit together to reveal some truth about the world. Knowledge hinges on an act of correlation and interpretation. At the top is wisdom, which has a moral component — it is the application of information worth remembering and knowledge that matters to understanding not only how the world works, but also how it should work. And that requires a moral framework of what should and shouldn't matter, as well as an ideal of the world at its highest potentiality. Such potentiality is opened to us through colourful and intimate stories. This is why the storyteller is all the more urgently valuable today.

A great storyteller — a journalist or filmmaker — helps people figure out not only what matters in the world, but also why it matters. "A great storyteller dances up the ladder of understanding, from information to knowledge to wisdom. Through symbol, metaphor, and association, the storyteller helps us interpret information, integrate it with our existing knowledge, and transmute that into wisdom" (Popova 2014).

Susan Sontag claimed: "reading sets standards." Storytelling not only sets standards but at its best, makes us want to live up to them, to transcend them. A great story, then, is not merely about providing information. It invites an expansion of understanding, a self-transcendence. "More than that, it plants the seed for it and makes it impossible to do anything but grow a new understanding — of the world, of our place in it, of ourselves, of some subtle or monumental aspect of existence" (Popova 2014). At a time when information is increasingly cheap and wisdom increasingly expensive, this gap is where the modern storyteller's value lives.

> Storytelling not only sets standards but at its best, makes us want to live up to them, to transcend them. A great story, then, is not merely about providing information. It invites an expansion of understanding, a self-transcendence.

Once we have built the ship, wisdom is what allows you to sail it without sinking, to protect it from the storm that creeps up from the horizon in the dead of the night, to point it just so that the wind breathes life into its sails. A great storyteller is the kindly captain who "sails her ship with tremendous wisdom and boundless courage; who points its nose in the direction of horizons and worlds chosen with unflinching idealism and integrity; who brings us somewhat closer to the answer, to our particular answer, to the question: Why are we here?"

As a collective family, human beings continue to answer this grand question through wise stories. As the philanthropist, Robert Redford says: "Storytelling is part of human continuity."

14

Our Common Story

How is the cosmos related to our idea of god? Raimon Panikkar, the Spanish-Indian thinker holds that when theology is divorced from cosmology, we no longer have a living god, but an idea of god. God then becomes a thought that can be accepted or rejected rather than the experience of divine ultimacy. Because theology has not developed in tandem with science (or science in tandem with theology) since the middle ages, we have an enormous gap between the transcendent dimension of human existence (the religious dimension) and the meaning of physical reality as science understands it (the material dimension). This gap underlies our global problems today, from the environmental crisis to economic disparity and the denigration of women," writes Richard Rohr, author of *Immortal Diamond*, in his Daily Meditations.

Stephen Hawking, the greatest theoretical physicist of our times believes humans have an innate drive to make sense of the world. He says: "Up to now, most scientists have been too occupied with the development of new theories that describe what the universe is to ask why. On the other hand, the people whose business it is to ask why, the philosophers [and, I would add, theologians] have not been able to keep up with the advance of scientific theory." He adds: "If we do discover a complete theory [of the universe], it should in time be understandable in broad principle by everyone, not just a few scientists. Then we shall all, philosophers, scientists, and just ordinary people, be able to take part in the discussion of the question of why it is that we and the universe exist. If we find the answer to that, it would be the ultimate triumph of human reason — for then we would know the mind of god."

Authors Mary Evelyn Tucker and Brian Swimme have helped our generation rediscover our common narrative, our shared cosmology. They write: "Just as we are realising the vast expanse of time that distinguishes the evolution of the universe over some 13.7 billion years, we are recognising how late is our arrival in this stupendous process. Just as we are becoming conscious that Earth took more than 4 billion years to bring forth this abundance of life, it is dawning on us how quickly we are foreshortening its future flourishing. We need, then, to step back, to assimilate our cosmological context." His conclusion is simple: "If scientific cosmology gives us an understanding of the origins and unfolding of the universe, reflection on scientific cosmology gives us a sense of our place in the universe" (Tucker and Swimme 2016).

The cosmology and theology of great saints and thinkers alike were so massive and so optimistic. For instance, Bonaventure's God was so much bigger and more glorious than someone to be afraid of or the one who punished bad guys — because his cosmos was itself huge, benevolent and coherent. Did his big God beget an equally big and generous cosmos? Or did his big cosmos imply a very big god? You can start on either side. For many in our time, an initial reverence for the universe leads them to reverence the infinity of mystery behind it. Those focused primarily on talking about God

"Just as we are realising the vast expanse of time that distinguishes the evolution of the universe over some 13.7 billion years, we are recognising how late is our arrival in this stupendous process. Just as we are becoming conscious that Earth took more than 4 billion years to bring forth this abundance of life, it is dawning on us how quickly we are foreshortening its future flourishing. We need, then, to step back, to assimilate our cosmological context."

somehow couldn't see a universe as holy, as big and as good as the one who supposedly created it. This "awe and reverence lead us to care for each other and our common home quickly, before we run out of time," wishes Richard Rohr. Cosmology and theology together can broaden our vision. So, we realise that "science and religion are long lost dance partners," as American author Rob Bell says.

Poetry and Language

15

Idleness May Be the Ideal Sometimes

Our struggle against the clock is ancient. As far back as the 2nd century BC, the Roman playwright Plautus lamented, "The gods confound the man who first found out how to distinguish the hours!" He railed against the sundial that "cut and hack my days so wretchedly."

The clock arrived when humans yearned for certainty and order, dividing time with increasing accuracy into neat units that could be accounted for, spent, saved or wasted. Yet, while our contemporary zeal to "get things done" might spur efficiency, it comes at a cost, claims Kerwin Jenkins, author of *All the Time in the World: A Book of Hours* (Jenkins 2013a) and *Encyclopedia of the Exquisite: An Anecdotal History of Elegant Delights* (Jenkins 2010), in *The New York Times* (Jenkins 2013).

Today, we are losing our "taste for unfragmented time," which the Scottish novelist, poet Robert Louis Stevenson cherished immensely. He relished a day "spent unaware of the hour, walking, pondering and lingering at the side of the road." During such moments, it seemed "almost as if the millennium were arrived, when we shall throw out clocks and watches over the housetop, and remember time and seasons no more," he wrote. "You have no idea, unless you have tried it, how endlessly long is a summer's day that you measure out only by hunger," and not by the clock.

The Enlightenment helped us to rediscover our penchant "to while away the hours in wonder." That is why the English philosopher Thomas Hobbes called curiosity the "singular passion" separating humans from animals. What pleasure we might know by letting curiosity have its way with us for an hour or two.

So, for many artists, doing nothing was a "fount of freedom." Stevenson again raised a rallying cry in *An Apology for Idlers* (1905), diagnosing extreme busyness as "a symptom of deficient vitality" (Jenkins 2013).

Our worship of time management robs us of the courage that aimless wanderers demonstrated when they stepped out of time. They risked reduced output for holistic liberation. For instance, Henry David Thoreau, whom Mahatma Gandhi admired so much, had sought solitude in the Massachusetts woods. The author of *Walden or, Life in the Woods* (1962), followed an unconventional timetable. Getting up to garden at 5 am and quitting by noon in order to pursue "other affairs," he liked to befriend squirrels or relax while reading *Homer* or the *Bhagavad Gita*. He chose to "live on the stretch" in order to better savour every moment. "I wanted to live deep and suck out all the marrow of life," he wrote.

Maybe we can relearn to let go of our urge to control everything by letting go of our certainties, so as to cherish life intimately.

Modern devices that constantly keep us on course, fixed in place and in time, do not enable us to relish creativity and "to suck out all the marrow of life." Instead they "ruin our ability to get lost, eradicating randomness and its magic in their wake," claims Jenkins. The stupefying modern obsession with productivity denies the whimsy and the freedom that living fully demands. So, she urges us to "dare to relax our grip on time for a day, or even for an hour, throwing clocks, watches and iPhones over the housetops, untethering ourselves solely for the thrill of not knowing what happens next"(Jenkins 2013).

Maybe we can relearn to let go of our urge to control everything by letting go of our certainties, so as to cherish life intimately. Genuine spirituality emerges when we are truly at home with ourselves and with the whole universe. Then we can let go of ourselves, to rediscover the beauty of randomness, the joy of getting lost and the thrill of letting go. That is delight, the ideal of idleness. That's true holidaying.

16

We must Behold the Beauty of Life

Newcomers are amazed to watch sculptures the size of buses walking along the sandy hills at Ypenburg in Netherlands. Made mostly from intricately conjoined plastic tubes, wood and sails, the many-legged skeletons, move so fluidly and autonomously. It seems they are almost alive!

Their maker, the Dutch artist Theo Jansen, certainly thinks so. "Since 1990, I have been occupied creating new forms of life," he says. "Eventually I want to put these animals out in herds on the beaches, so they will live their own lives" (Jaber 2014).

Called Strandbeests, they are elaborate, beautiful and inanimate contraptions. They are definitely not alive. But science cannot define life. A precise, universally accepted definition of life does not exist. To compensate, modern textbooks point to characteristics that supposedly distinguish the living from the inanimate, the most important of which are organisation, growth, reproduction and evolution.

Crystals, for example, are highly organised; they grow; and they faithfully replicate their structures, but we do not think of them as alive. Similarly, certain computer programs known as "digital organisms" can reproduce, mate and evolve, but ushering such softwares through the gates to the kingdom of life makes many people uncomfortable. Conversely, some organisms — such as gummy bear-shaped microanimals — can "enter a period of extreme dormancy during which they stop eating, growing and changing in any way for years at a time, yet are still regarded as living organisms," writes Ferris Jabr, a freelancer writer and associate editor of Scientific American (Jaber 2014). Jabr takes the case if a virus — a bit of DNA or RNA encased in protein that hijacks a cell to make copies of itself. Viruses are incredibly efficient reproducers and they certainly evolve — much faster than most creatures. Yet biologists do not know whether they are living, non-living or something in between.

The same is true, though, of many larger parasites we consider living. Bloodthirsty intestinal worms, vines that suck the sap from other plants, fungi that extrude filamentous antlers of flame orange through the shells of spiders they have killed — all are just as dependent on their hosts to reproduce and evolve as is a virus. It is truly difficult to distinguish living from non-living. Not only is defining life futile, but it is "also unnecessary to understanding how living things work," claims Jabr. All observable matter is, at its most fundamental level, an arrangement of atoms and their constituent particles. These associations range in complexity from something as simple as, say, a single molecule of water to something as astonishingly intricate as an ant colony. All the proposed features of life are processes that appear at many different regions of this great spectrum of matter. There is no precise threshold between living and non-living things. Some things we regard as inanimate are capable of some processes we want to make exclusive to life. And some things we say are alive get along just fine without some of those processes. Yet we wish to see matter divided into life and nonlife. Therein lies the ambiguity, frailty, complexity and beauty of being alive (Jaber 2014)!

Behold the complex beauty and be! Life – together with non-life – in an exclamation!

The real reason Strandbeest enchants us, claims Jabr, is because it is so complex and, in its complexity, beautiful. He invites us to watch a Strandbeest's sail "undulate in the wind, its gears begin to turn, its legs bend and extend in sync over and over — so dauntless, so determined." He pleads: Just look at it go. Behold the complex beauty and be! Life – together with non-life – in an exclamation!

17

Turns out, You Can Cultivate Compassion

Can we actively foster compassion? Until now, little was scientifically known about the human potential to cultivate compassion that motivates altruistic behaviour.

A new study by researchers at the University of Wisconsin-Madison shows that adults can be trained to be more compassionate. The study, reported in *ScienceDaily*, investigates whet-her training adults in compassion can result in greater altruistic behaviour and related changes in neural systems underlying compassion.

"Can compassion be trained and learned in adults? Can we become more caring if we practice that mindset?" asked Helen Weng, lead author of the study (Association for Psychological Science. 2013). The study points to an affirmative answer.

In the study, the investigators trained young adults to engage in compassion meditation, according to the Buddhist tradition. In the meditation, participants envisioned a time when someone has suffered and then practiced wishing that his or her suffering was relieved. They repeated phrases to help them focus on compassion such as, "May you be free from suffering. May you have joy and ease."

Participants practiced with different categories of people, first starting with a loved one, someone whom they easily felt compassion for, like a friend or family member. Later, they practiced compassion for themselves and then, a stranger. Finally, they practiced compassion for someone they actively had conflict with called the "difficult person," such as a troublesome co-worker or roommate.

"Using this systematic approach, we found that people can actually build up their compassion 'muscle' and respond to others' suffering with care and a desire to help," Weng claimed (Association for Psychological Science. 2013). Compassion training was compared to a control group that learned cognitive reappraisal, a technique where people learn to reframe their thoughts to feel less negative. "We found that people trained in compassion were more likely to spend their own money altruistically to help someone who was treated unfairly," Weng says.

"We wanted to see what changed inside the brains of people who gave more to someone in need. How are they responding to suffering differently now?" asks Weng (Association for Psychological Science. 2013). The study measured changes in brain responses using functional magnetic resonance imaging before and after training. In the MRI scanner, participants viewed images of human suffering, such as a crying child or a burn victim, and generated feelings of compassion towards the people using their practiced skills. The control group was exposed to the same images, and asked to recast them in a more positive light as in reappraisal.

The researchers measured how much brain activity had changed from the beginning to the end of training. They found that people who were the most altruistic after compassion training were the ones who showed the most brain changes when viewing human suffering. People "learn to regulate their emotions and approach people's suffering with caring and want to help rather than turn away," explains Weng.

> Unless we learn to be genuinely compassionate to ourselves, to the animal world and to the earth, our very survival is at stake. We have the spiritual and scientific resources for such compassionate life and now is the time to draw on them.

Weng thinks that compassion training can help the general population. Unless we learn to be genuinely compassionate to ourselves, to the animal world and to the earth, our very survival is at stake. We have the spiritual and scientific resources for such compassionate life and now is the time to draw on them.

18

Is it too Difficult to Forgive and Forget?

People hurt us most of the times. Sometimes we are hurt very badly. But can we really forgive them? Even if we forgive, can we overcome the negative emotion, haunting thoughts, or vengeful impulses and be truly magnanimous to those who have hurt us?

Forgiving and forgetting are tightly entwined in human culture, but it's only in the past decade or so that researchers have begun to systematically relate forgiving and forgetting. Why is it that some of us find it easier to forgive and forget than others? These issues were the concern of a team of psychological scientists at the University of St Andrews, Scotland. Saima Noreen, school of psychology and neuroscience, University of St Andrews, suspected that the link between forgiving and forgetting might be the "mind's executive control system," specifically the ability to keep upsetting memories out of consciousness. She and colleagues tested this connection and reported their findings in *Psychological Science* (University of St Andrews. 2014).

For the experiment, they recruited volunteers and measured their general tendency to forgive others' wrongdoings. Creating various scenarios depicting hypothetical wrongdoings — slander, infidelity, or theft, among others — the recruits were closely monitored. In some cases, the transgressor was a friend; other times a partner, parent or colleague.

The scenarios always had consequences — and there was always an attempt at making amends. For example, one scenario might go like this: Your professor doesn't believe you when you say you didn't plagiarise your work. You are expelled from the university, but later your professor realises you were telling the truth and tries to get you reinstated. The volunteers reacted to each of these hypothetical scenarios in various ways: How serious was the offence? How hurtful? How sympathetic were you toward the transgressor? And can you forgive or forget the incident.

Later, the volunteers took part in a memory test, in which they actively tried to forget words associated with the incident. The idea was to see if the act of forgiving increased the victims' ability to put the misfortunes out of awareness.

The "ability to forget unpleasantness is linked to actual acts of forgiving, not just a propensity to be gracious."

The study narrated by Wray Herbert (2010), author of *On Second Thought: Outsmarting Your Mind's Hard-Wired Habits* in *The Huffington Post*, shows a clear connection. When victims had forgiven their transgressor, they were much better at suppressing — intentionally forgetting — words linked to the transgressions. But when the victims had not found it in themselves to forgive, they were much less successful at suppressing the unwanted memories. What's more, the "ability to forget unpleasantness is linked to actual acts of forgiving, not just a propensity to be gracious." Not everyone has it in their hearts to forgive so readily. But it's possible, the scientists conclude, that forgiving and forgetting reinforce one another in the human mind. Even if forgiveness is effortful at first, people who manage it may be better at setting bitter thoughts aside, and this forgetting may in turn provide an effective coping strategy, enabling people to move on and to forgive (University of St Andrews. 2014).

We need forgiveness both at the individual and societal level. The study suggests that forgiveness can be learnt and psychologically fostered. Humanity needs such ability to forgive and to forget, without ignoring, the harm done to us. For the survival and well-being of our human society, forgiveness is necessary. The fundamental basis for forgiveness is the deep conviction that the wrongs we have done can be corrected and overcome by a greater power — the divine.

19

Generosity Leads to Win-Win Situations

"Nowadays people know the price of everything and the value of nothing," moaned Oscar Wilde (Wilde 1998: 15), world-renowned Irish playwright more 100 years ago. Now when we look at our own lives, we realise that we have put price tags on things that Wilde even in his wildest dreams could not have seen coming.

For example, today for $10, a company can purchase the right to emit a metric tonne of carbon dioxide into the atmosphere. For $7,500, one can hire a human being to be a guinea pig in risky drug trials. We've somehow managed to put a price tag on life, death and almost everything in between. So, what happens to the priceless?, asks Pavithra Mehta, co-author of *Infinite Vision* (Shenoy and Mehta 2011).

She adds: "We live in a time where we have mastered the art of "liking" each other on Facebook but have forgotten the art of loving each other in real life." Disconnection with fellow-human beings has become "a growing epidemic." It is not limited to teenagers, but to the whole human family and especially to the workplace. According to one reputed study, about 70 per cent of people are emotionally disconnected at work. We have even given a price tag for that disconnection. It's estimated to be $300 billion in lost productivity annually, due to such disconnection. So, disconnection today has become "not just a social or spiritual problem," asserts Mehta. It's also a business problem, an economic problem (Mehta 2014).

Making meaningful products is necessary, but not enough. She adds, "Our purpose doesn't lie in our commodities, it lies in our sense of communion" (Mehta 2014). Our meaning lies not primarily in our priced products, but in our valuable presence. We can't put a price on a smile, the cold wind or our hopes and aspirations. Compassion, empathy, generosity, trust and love are priceless and precious gifts. So, can we bring them back today?

Many great people have practiced radically generous acts that have transformed the world. Leaders like Mahatma Gandhi, Mother Teresa, Martin Luther King, Nelson Mandela and numerous unsung heroes were the people who believed that when we change ourselves, we could fundamentally change the world. The seeds of such generosity and self-giving, which Mehta calls "giftivism," lie in each of us. But to tap into it, we have to do something all these people did. We have to upturn one of the core assumptions of economics — the assumption that people always act to maximise self-interest, or that we are inherently selfish beings — to enable a new way of living (Mehta 2014).

> "Nowadays people know the price of everything and the value of nothing."
> (Oscar Wilde)

One suggestion that Mehta makes is to move from the attitude of consumption to contribution. In large cities, we encounter 5,000 ads a day. The marketplace goads us for endless consumption. But the truth is we're hard wired for contribution. When people give to good causes, it can trigger the same pleasure response in the brain that doing something nice for themselves does! We can start doing small acts of kindness, such as buying coffee for a stranger at a café, or giving your seat in the train to some unknown person. These small, counterculture gestures light up the giver and receiver. Everybody wins because generosity is not a zero-sum game.

Imagine a world where people are continually reaching out to each other in this priceless way! Every moment becomes a gift. Soon we realise that our actions begin to catalyse a rich network of ripples, which tap into the joy of purpose. We move from price tags to the priceless values that we possess, individually and collectively.

20

An Economic and Spiritual Language

It is rare that an economic treatise becomes a bestseller. French economist Thomas Piketty has authored an intellectually hefty book, *Capital in the Twenty-First Century*, which has given rise to so much discussion, making it a bestseller (Piketty 2014).

Its main insight may be summed up in the simple formula: $r > g$. Here, r stands for the annual rate of return on capital (including profits, dividends, interest, rents and other income from capital, expressed as a percentage of total value). The other variable, g stands for the rate of growth of the economy.

The 700-page book takes us through complex economic analysis. But the profound implication is clear: Capital is growing faster than national income implying that inequality is widening. Piketty's volume, translated from the French, has provoked wide discussion. For example, US President Barrack Obama called income inequality the "defining challenge of our time." For many thinkers, vast extremes of wealth are a matter of justice or absence of it. There is a general recognition that economic extremes foster instability and are unsustainable over the long run. Piketty has some relevant insights on inequality. "According to the best available estimates, global output grew at an average annual rate of 1.6 per cent between 1700 and 2012." At the same time, "the average long-run rate of return on stocks is 7-8 per cent in many countries. Investments in real estate and bonds frequently return 3-4 per cent." This implies that concentrations of wealth keep on growing faster than income and income disparity keeps on widening.

Further Piketty mentions two phenomena that accelerate even further the mechanisms of disparity. The first is the tendency of capital to yield higher rates of return the more one owns. The second is the demographic trends in developed countries. Here, the reduced population growth means that wealth is not divided among four, five or seven offspring, but among two or three, thus preserving intergenerational concentration of capital, which will last for many more years (Piketty 2014).

Therefore, Piketty holds that "at the beginning of the 1970s, the total value of private wealth (net of debt) stood between two and three and a half years of national income in all the rich countries, on all continents. 40 years later, in 2010, private wealth represented between four and seven years of national income in all the countries under study." In other words, the ratio of wealth to income increases over time. According to Piketty, that ratio "could approach 700 per cent before the end of the 21st century."

"The history of inequality is shaped by the way economic, social, and political actors view what is just and what is not, as well as by the relative power of those actors and the collective choices that result."

Nevertheless, Piketty rejects economic determinism. So he says: "The history of inequality is shaped by the way economic, social, and political actors view what is just and what is not, as well as by the relative power of those actors and the collective choices that result." American author Earl Pike opines that "*Capital in the Twenty-First Century* is strong on diagnosis, weaker on remedies." Noting how our intellectual conversation is now a conversation about economics, another author Benjamin Wallace-Wells asserts, "It isn't just that economics is the topic we are most interested in; economics, increasingly, is the only language that we're speaking" (Piketty 2014).

The larger question is: Is it true also in spirituality? Does spirituality also speak the language of economics? Though as spiritual persons, we are convinced that each person deserves respect and financial independence, do we create such a possibility? Could we enable a society where there is more of economic and spiritual egalitarianism? Could we ever say bye to spiritual intolerance and economic inequality?

21

Poetry Often Links Culture and Society

Does poetry matter? Writing an opinion column in *The New York Times*, poet David Biespiel relates poems to the aspirations of collective humanity. He claims that every society we have ever lived in has had poetry and should the day come that poetry suddenly disappears in the morning, someone, somewhere, will reinvent it by evening (Beispiel 2014).

Since ancient times, as long as we've had language, poetry has ritualised human life. It has "dramatised and informed us with metaphors and figures of feeling and thought, mysteries and politics, birth and death, and all the occasions we experience between womb and tomb."

Poetic utterance ritualises how we come to knowledge. In the same way that poetry illuminates our individual lives, poems also help us understand ourselves as a culture. Or at least they spur us to ask the questions. He adds: "Poetic utterance mythologises our journey of being. Poetic utterance tells and interprets our stories. Poetic utterance shapes our perspective of the mysteries of the present moment and helps us imagine the next one" (Beispiel 2014).

He cites Walt Whitman, the American poet and journalist who invites us to join the communion between poet and human aspiration by asserting: "And what I assume you shall assume, for every atom belonging to me as good belongs to you."

Biespiel elaborates: "In this way, poetry connects us to our past, and poets unmask both private and civic memories, dreams, and urgencies. By harmonising the body with the mind, serving both young and old, poetry is a guide to deliver us into a fresh engagement with our inner lives and with modernity."

> Poetry has ritualised human life, "dramatised and informed us with metaphors and figures of feeling and thought, mysteries and politics, birth and death, and all the occasions we experience between womb and tomb."

Thus, he pleads that poetry really matters in human life. "If we care about order and disorder, then poetry matters because it is the art of the utterance of beauty and the grotesque." He goes on: "If we care about the deepest aspirations of men and women across every community and culture, language and race, then poetry is always relevant because it is the art of the utterance of what we share in our innermost psyches" (Beispiel 2014).

He links culture and society through poetry. Since they existed both "before we live and after we die, poetry is a link to our passage through our own time." The perspectives of the poets are important in relating us to our past and future.

In this way, poetry is related to the deep interconnectedness between human beings. "We know that human beings are intrinsically connected to one another in how we assert our being. When we read a poem, we are in the presençe of this link. We are open to the metaphors of our shared natures," he holds.

Beispiel goes on: "A poem orients us in both our inner and outer existence. No matter what language we speak, we follow the guidance of poetry to better perceive sorrow and radiance, love and hatred, violence and wonder. No matter what continent we call home, we read poetry to restrict us in time and to aspire toward timelessness — whether we are in our most vibrant cities or in the remote woods" (Beispiel 2014).

To the question, "Does poetry matter?" his answer is a definite "yes." To the question, "Can poetry be more relevant?" he answers negatively. "It is the song of song, the language of language, the utterance of utterance and the spirit of spirit." So, poetry cannot be judged by its relevance. It matters very much. It relates us to the whole reality. So, like prayer, poetry cannot be measured by its relevance.

Spirituality and Service

22

When Regrets of the Dying Teach Us to Live

Elders in every society carry with them some wisdom, which they can meaningfully transmit to the younger generation. Bronnie Ware is an Australian nurse, who spent many years working in palliative care caring for those who were dying. From her experience with the elders, she published the book *The Top Five Regrets of the Dying* (Ware 2012).

Regrets can be seen as something that is good if they provide us with insight into what we can change for the better. Here we use these regrets as the North Star to help guide ourselves towards a more fulfilling life.

The first regret of the dying is: "I wish I'd had the courage to live a life true to myself, not the life others expected of me" (Goldstein 2013). From the time we are born, we look to our parents and significant others to teach us the rules of this world and to guide our expectations about how we should or shouldn't act. It is common that we look up to others to guide how we should dress, speak, act, and even what kind of profession we should be in. It would be better if we get in touch with what seems right to ourselves and live an authentic life.

The second regret is: "I wish I hadn't worked so hard." Without work we cannot live. Sometimes we work too much out of routine, other times from other people's expectations and sometimes as an addictive behaviour to avoid discomfort. But, we need to realise that there are things that may be more valuable and that nourish us more than merely working (Goldstein 2013).

Another regret is: "I wish I'd had the courage to express my feelings." Whether at work, or in a relationship, normally we tend to be evasive or even reticent with regards to our feelings. Standing in an authentic life means becoming aware of and expressing our feelings. Learning to let others know that we love them can create deeper connections. Learning how to become more aware of our emotions and express them in a skilful way can help us feel more connected, self-reliant and happy.

The fourth regret is: "I wish I had stayed in touch with my friends." Without a doubt, at the crux of feeling happy and fulfilled in life, is having nurturing relationships. We need to make it a priority to make relationships an integral part of our day-to-day life. That will help us remain connected with others (Goldstein 2013).

The last regret is: "I wish that I had let myself be happier." Bronnie Ware said that many people did not notice until the end of life that happiness is a choice. With awareness we can make conscious choices about what nourishes us and what depletes us. What beliefs we want to invest in and which ones we don't. We may get hooked into states of high stress, anxiety, depression and even trauma reactions, but at some point, we get to choose how we want to relate to them and this may help us ride them with more grace.

These five regrets are like the North Star that urges us to remain true to our own selves and find fulfilment. As psychologist Elisha Goldstein, PhD, and author of *The Now Effect* (Goldstein 2012) observes, that we may veer off the path. But when we notice the star, we can always come back to it. It is never too late to start living our lives intensely, meaningfully and happily. These regrets can help us choose the life we want to lead for ourselves.

> Regrets can be seen as something that is good if they provide us with insight into what we can change for the better. These regrets as the North Star to help guide ourselves towards a more fulfilling life.

23

What Christmas Really Teaches Us

Christmas is the celebration of peace, good will and reconciliation. According to the Biblical account, the first announcement of Jesus' birth was made by angels to shepherds outside of Bethlehem. They sang: Glory to God in the highest, and on earth peace, good will toward all men.

Christmas is also a feast of feeling at home. In this feast, we recall that God came to the earth and made it his home. So we are called to feel fully at home in this world. That is why Christmas has become a family feast, where members celebrate memories together in a homily ambience.

At the same time, we may wonder where we find real peace. The Christmas message of "peace on earth" seems to be very elusive today. Here it may be useful to recall the story of Jesus, the Prince of Peace. Jesus came to earth in a peaceful way as a baby in a modest circumstance of a manger and proceeded to live a humble life. He healed many people and taught that God himself is love and he is on their side. He urged us to love one another. Of course, he was not talking of self-serving kind of love, but a forgiving, sacrificing and joyful love. He invited us even to love our own enemies. But he himself paid the price for the values he lived by. Tragically, the prince of peace was scorned at and tortured. One who forgave his enemies was put to death. Jesus embraced this broken world, tried to bring about peace through committed love, failed, and in his very failure, he succeeded.

Through his message, life and death, he reconciled us with one another and with god. Because of his totally selfless love and purity of heart, Christians believe that in Jesus, God revealed himself to us. They hold that Jesus is truly God taking upon himself our limitations and living with us. In this way, Jesus restored our broken relationship with God and to one another. He came to offer us the experience of wholeness and unconditional love.

God experiences our struggles and walks with us. He knows our strife and our longing — both individual and collective — for peace. Christian faith is the assertion that God is the answer to this deepest human longing for wholeness and peace. By living like Jesus, everyone is assured of the genuine peace. It may not comfortable peace of the "bed of roses" type. Surely not the peace of bon-bons; rather, it is the peace that comes through struggle and turmoil. The peace is encountering god, who dares to walk with us, toil with us and even fail with us.

Such a human-god assures that peace is already in us and peace will be our destiny. Not merely the individual "feel-at-ease" kind of peace, but a collective peace where we all live as brothers and sisters.

So, the message of Christmas does not make life easy or undisturbed. Rather, Christmas invites to walk in faith, hope and love so that collectively and together with the loving God we can experience peace.

So, Christmas is true encounter — with God and with others. With the best and the worst in our human hearts. It is reaching out to our enemies and engaging ourselves in real struggle for brotherhood and love. "We consider Christmas as the encounter, the great encounter, the historical encounter, the decisive encounter, between God and mankind. He who has faith knows this truly; let him rejoice," holds Pope Paul VI. So, the message of the child Jesus is that peace — in our hearts and on earth — is achievable through sustained work, purity of heart and by self-surrender.

So the message of the child Jesus is that peace — in our hearts and on earth — is achievable through sustained work, purity of heart and by self-surrender.

24

The Synthetic Allure of Narcissistic Spirituality

Following Rabbi Alan Lurie, the author of *Five Minutes on Mondays: Finding Unexpected, Purpose, Peace and Fulfilment at Work* (Lurie 2009), we may define spirituality as, "the experience of a transformative connection." To elaborate: spirituality is experienced and thus, is not a concept or construct. It transforms us. It changes how we act, think and feel. And it is a connection, a profound contact with something or someone outside of our selves.

All three of these components are essential for spiritual vitality, but the most essential aspect is the connection or relationship between one and the 'divine', or between one and others. All spiritual practices are designed to facilitate these connections. But there are associated dangers. Alan Lurie warns in *The Huffington Post* that at times, spiritual practices may become narcissistic, "when the ego-self hijacks the process and assumes that it is the object of self-love, becoming enamoured of looking in the mirror and claiming that its reflection is the true-self" (Lurie 2011). Then we forget that the purpose of spirituality is to become more open in interactions with others so that we open our hearts with humility. Instead we assume a position of superiority — exactly what the ego desires for its safety. Thus, "spiritual narcissism sees self-love as the end goal," he affirms. In spiritual narcissism, spirituality becomes an object of attainment, much like fame, wealth, an expensive car or a sexy body.

> "When two people relate to each other authentically and humanly, God is the electricity that surges between them."
> (Martin Buber)

Spiritual narcissism creates the pretence of holiness as "an ego strategy to mask insecurity," that receives approval, or avoids struggle and growth. "I'm a spiritual person," it proclaims proudly. "I travel to alternate realities, see auras, heal chakras, predict the future, talk to spirits and angels, manipulate energies, meditate for three daily, harness the powers of the universe to attract success. The truth is that I'm more evolved than you!" (Lurie 2011).

Genuine spirituality, on the other hand, makes us compassionate, enabling us to be more sensitive to the feeling of others, encouraging an open stance of courage "where we can drop our protective shields and accept the vulnerability to be seen as we are." Narcissistic sensitivity, however, is focussed "solely on the subtle nuances of one's own internality, and resists looking at hard, uncomfortable truths that may upset the self image," claims Lurie. One who is narcissistically sensitive is easily offended by the "coarseness" of others, seeks to make the environment change to align with the contours of one's needs, and gets angry when this does not happen.

The desire to control others in order to create a "perfect" environment that nurtures our selfish sensitivities is a calling card of spiritual narcissism. "It is not a spiritual feat to feel equanimity only when everything is going exactly as one would like." He adds, "True spirituality takes place in the holy messiness of the world, in open-hearted relationship with others, and in a kind smile to one who accidentally stepped on your foot" (Lurie 2011). In that moment of connection, the annoyance we feel actually become wake up calls pulling us out of our self-involvement and in to relationship.

Sometimes spirituality may become too self-centred, self-protective and selfish, taking us away from others. However, once we understand how we are "tempted to use the guise of spirituality to shield us from criticism, impress others and make us feel wise, its appeal begins to loosen, and we even find the humour in this upside-down dynamic." As philosopher Martin Buber wrote, "When two people relate to each other authentically and humanly, God is the electricity that surges between them."

25

Genuine Progress is also Spiritual

We live in a society that measures 'progress' in terms of material or economic growth. As we run up against the material limits of growth and move into an era where sustainability is key to our survival as a species, this historically narrow but rapidly successful view of progress could prevent us from realising the larger vision of human advancement.

The eminent historian Arnold Toynbee invested a lifetime studying the rise and fall of civilisations. In conducting his wide-ranging scholarship, Toynbee found a strong connection between simplicity and human progress. He summarised the essence of a civilisation's growth in a single law that he called "The law of progressive simplification." He wrote that the progress of a civilisation could not be measured accurately by its conquest of land and people. Instead, the true measure of growth lies in a civilisation's ability to transfer increasing amounts of energy and attention from the material side of life to the non-material side — areas such as personal growth, family relationships, cultivating of arts, theatre, music, citizenship and democracy (Toynbee and Somervell. 1947).

To clarify this, Toynbee invented the word "etherialisation" to describe the process whereby, over time, we humans learn to accomplish the same, or even greater, results using less time and energy. Architect and futurist Buckminster Fuller used the term "ephemeralisation" to describe a similar process (Elgin 2011).

Material ephemeralisation is evident in many areas of our lives. For example, computers have evolved from room-sized giants to slim laptops with vastly more computing power. Libraries are being transformed from massive buildings that warehouse millions of books to small computer chips that can store — and retrieve — an even greater volume of knowledge.

> As a species, we can grow in empathy and compassion, in our intellectual understanding, and in creative expressions such as music and poetry and in spiritual longing.

Integrating the historical insights of Toynbee and material insights of Fuller, Duane Elgin, activist author of *Voluntary Simplicity*, (Elgin 1993) redefined progress as follows: "Progress is a two-fold process involving the simultaneous refinement of the material and non-material aspects of life." With ephemeralisation, the material side of life grows lighter, stronger and more eco-friendly in production, consumption and recycling. At the same time, the non-material side of life grows in vitality, expressiveness and insight. "Ephemeralisation involves the co-evolution of inner and outer aspects of life in balance with one another," says Elgin (Elgin 2011).

Elgin holds that as a species, we can grow in empathy and compassion, in our intellectual understanding, and in creative expressions such as music and poetry and in spiritual longing.

Progressive simplification or ephemeralism is a "co-evolutionary approach to living that invites us to continuously balance two aspects of life — maintaining ourselves and surpassing ourselves." Philosopher Simone de Beauvoir clarifies this: "Life is occupied in both perpetuating itself and in surpassing itself; if all it does is maintain itself, then living is only not dying" (cited in Elgin 2011).

Therefore, if we seek only to maintain ourselves, then no matter how grand our style of living might be, we are doing little more than surviving. On the other hand, if we strive only to surpass ourselves without securing the material foundation that supports our lives, then our physical existence is in jeopardy and the opportunity to find meaning becomes little more than a utopian dream. Thus, genuine progress is a creative interplay between material well-being and spiritual maturity.

26

Celebrating Material Possessions Mindfully

In our consumerist and materialistic culture, we are used to things being routinely discarded or replaced. "The problem with our society is not that it values material things too much, but that it doesn't value them enough," claims the award winning journalist Nick Thorpe writing in *AEON Magazine*.

So professor David MacKay, chief scientific adviser, UK department of energy and climate change, bemoans "the way in which economic activity and growth currently is coupled to buying lots of stuff and then throwing it away." According to data collected by the Global Footprint Network, it takes the biosphere a year to produce what human beings consume in roughly eight months; a situation that is surely unsustainable. And yet we persevere with what the British psychologist Michael Eysenck calls the 'hedonic treadmill,' hoping that "the spike of satisfaction from our next purchase will somehow prove less transitory than the last." In fact, the opposite is true, asserts Thorpe (Thorpe 2016).

In *The High Price of Materialism* (2002), American psychologist Tim Kasser shows that the cravings of consumerism tend to make us more miserable. Though most of us know this instinctively, we do not know how to remedy this troubled relationship with material possessions. One knee-jerk reaction is to cultivate a sort of blanket disdain for consumer goods. "And yet when applied to my whole life, such a hair-shirted response is ultimately as unsustainable as the position it challenges," according to Thorpe.

If our consumer culture sometimes resembles "a bulimic binge in which we taste and then spew back things that never quite nourish us," the opposite "ascetic, anorexic alternative of rejecting materialism altogether will leave us equally starved." We need a new attitude to the material possession enabling us to celebrate them mindfully. In *Vibrant Matter: A Political Ecology of Things*, Jane Bennett (2010) writes that if we paid attention to the "aliveness of matter," we wouldn't be so careless with our material possessions. But the "disjointedness of hyper-consumerism conceals the continuing life of objects, built anonymously in distant factories and eventually left to leech chemicals into landfill" does not connect us with the objects we own. Instead of "litter, rubbish, trash" or "the recycling," if we perceive matter as positive and encounter "an accumulating pile of lively and potentially dangerous matter," then our consumption pattern will change (Thorpe 2016).

In its forceful and relevant manifesto Andrew Simms, activist and author of *The New Materialism*, relates genuine materialism to economics (Simms and Potts 2012). He explains that creating a society in which "things last longer and are endlessly re-used will necessarily entail a major shift to the services that keep things going, thereby creating employment to replace lost manufacturing or retail output." In the same vein, Herman Daly, editor of *Ecological Economics*, calls for the "subtle and complex economics of maintenance, qualitative improvements, sharing, frugality, and adaptation to natural limits. It is an economics of better, not bigger." Such an economy is based on a relationship that values and cherishes material things. So, we need

The "disjointedness of hyper-consumerism conceals the continuing life of objects, built anonymously in distant factories and eventually left to leech chemicals into landfill" does not connect us with the objects we own.

to move away from crass consumerism to concerned materialism (Thorpe 2016).

Can we evolve a spirituality that helps us value and cherish material things? Can we learn to consume, but respectfully and reverentially, so that we can lead happy and sustainable lives? Can we celebrate our material possession knowing that they are truly part of us?

27

Attain Liberation through the Body

Christians have just celebrated the feast of the resurrection of Jesus, their founder. Resurrection of Jesus is the "foundational event" of Christianity. What is its significance for us today? Christians shape their life and destiny on this fundamental experience that Jesus is not dead but is alive. In other words, Christians believe that the painful and debasing death on the cross is not the end of Christ and of humanity.

Right from the beginning, Christians have proclaimed the "resurrection of the body." It may be remembered that the other great feast of Christians, Christmas, is also closely connected to body. Christmas is the feast which proclaims that God has really taken upon the body — flesh and blood — of human being and has lived among us.

Though many people imagine that resurrection is "liberation from the body," it is in fact liberation through the body. The Christian experience is that Jesus lived a life of unconditional love, suffered tremendously and died a miserable death. He suffered physically, emotionally and even spiritually. At the cross, he felt forsaken and abandoned even by god. So his end was despicable and shameful.

After such a death, his body was buried. And on the third day, Jesus rose again in his "transformed body." So, the Christians do not believe in the resurrection of the soul, but that of the mortal body which has been transformed. This implies that for Christians, the frail and fragile body is very important in attaining one's liberation.

It also implies that along with our physical and corruptible bodies, the material things are also religiously significant. This means that our physical human condition on earth is very necessarily our way of holiness. So our failures, disappointments, success and hopes are all meaningful steps towards liberation. Thus, our relationships, concerns, struggles and successes have a relative and necessary worth, in our final fulfilment. Though they will be purified and transformed, they are very much part of our destiny.

In that sense, Christianity is a "materialistic religion," which urges us to take the world seriously (Augsburger 1989). Of course, our material well-being is not absolute. But they are crucial in attaining our own liberation. Our struggle for a more egalitarian society, and our commitment to the poor are a necessary part of realising our fullness. In this sense, the Christian way of achieving liberation is in and through the body or the material world. This implies that as religious people we have to commit ourselves to bettering the lot of our neighbours. Only by visualising a "new creation," can each one attain our own liberation. As such liberation is not just an individual affair but a collective one, where the whole material things and historical events are necessarily part of.

> Human body, material things as well as our political and historical experiences are sacred, though not divine. They are part of god's plan of enabling our collective and holistic liberation.

This implies that body, material things as well as our political and historical experiences are sacred, though not divine. They are part of god's plan of enabling our collective and holistic liberation. Our painful and shameful experiences contribute to our fullness too. They become an integral part of our human experience and liberation. So, even the smallest things that we achieve or fail to achieve are part of the divine plan to realise our own liberation. Our liberation comes through the limited bodily experience that we all share collectively.

Thus, the Christian experience of the resurrection is the proclamation of the power of love — love of our neighbour, love of own fragile bodies, love of the world we live in. Such a love stems from God and leads to god. Ultimately, such an unconditional love triumphs and is all-inclusive.

28

Finding Spirituality in Ordinary Things

Polly Campbell, a renowned author who specialises in spirituality, describes spirituality as "a profound physical, emotional and intellectual awareness of her core self, as the connection to all that she is." In her book *Imperfect Spirituality: Extraordinary Enlightenment for Ordinary People* (Campbell 2012), she elaborates: "Spirituality is about living with this awareness (of spirit) in deep relationship with yourself — the self that is both created by and connected to the universal source of all that is. From this place you recognise that everything is interconnected. We are all one."

Margarita Tartakovsky, an associate editor at *Psych Central blog*, summarises Campbell's vision of spirituality, which is not "something to develop; it's who we are" (Tartakovsky 2016). For Campbell, spirituality is "part of our makeup, just like brown eyes and curly hair." So, she tells us: "What we need to do is uncover it and remember who we are." To be spiritual is to be in touch with the higher energy that pervades everywhere. She asserts: "When you touch your spirit from this place of knowing, you are then guided by this higher energy, instead of ego. This energy is fuelled by love and compassion, gratitude and expansion. It is not about gossip or image or control. It isn't about being right or better than."

To realise such spiritual state, some spiritual practices are helpful. Practices such as mindfulness, meditation and even exercise can help us remember who we are. Even ordinary activities like

> Having fun is a spiritual state. "Do the things that ignite and inspire you."

cooking or playing with one's kids can be spiritual practices "if done with conscious awareness," can lead us to deep spiritual awareness. Campbell's spiritual practice helps her be more present, appreciative and grateful. It helps her connect to the moments of her day. It also helps her be more grounded and resilient. "Life is more fun" (Tartakovsky 2016).

She recommends some personal practice that enhances our spiritual openness. The first is to become aware. "Become aware of what you're putting into your mind, heart and into your day," said Campbell. "Notice the routines you're in and how you're thinking of them." Notice how you relate to your loved ones, such as your partner and kids.

Campbell suggests that we practice this awareness during the transitions of the day, such as when we wake up, eating lunch and before going to bed. "Three times a day, stop and notice where you are," she advises us. We need to simply notice without judging.

Another helpful practice is to write regularly: Journaling can help us gain clarity and connect to our higher spirit. She suggests answering these questions: "What did I learn about myself today? What is important to me now? What do I value now?" In Imperfect Spirituality, she includes these questions: "How did I behave compassionately today? What do I most need to know about my life and my purpose? How did I live close to my values today?" She suggests writing about our dreams, concerns, feelings and creating gratitude lists (Tartakovsky 2016).

A third practice is to be curious: "Curiosity and novelty are huge ways in to discover our spiritual essence," Campbell holds. This can include doing one different thing each day, such as "coming home a new way, or reading a book from a genre you never read." In fact, she points out that having fun is a spiritual state. So she suggests: "Do the things that ignite and inspire you," since they take our "mind to different tools and levels of consciousness" (Tartakovsky 2016).

Can we connect ourselves to the higher energy and find spiritual depth in simple, ordinary and even imperfect things?

29

India's Greatest Gift to the World

What we hear most often about India these days is its "extraordinary leap into the modern world, her burgeoning prosperity, and her enormous contribution to the global economy." And while this is all true, Andrew Cohen, a renowned spiritual teacher and advocate of "Evolutionary Enlightenment," thinks that India's greatest gift to the world still remains what it is most famous for: the gift of spirituality (Cohen 2013).

Though "India's ochre-coloured holy men are often seen as clichés and holdovers from a bygone era" in the west, he believes that the spiritual heart "of ancient and still mysterious land" is "still alive and bursting at the seams with mystical potency." Writing in Patheos (a website that talks about various religions), he acknowledges that the situation is changing rapidly. For instance, yoga, once a lofty spiritual practice only for initiates, has become a mainstream commercial enterprise all over the world. Newspapers have countless articles about the health benefits of yoga postures and breathing techniques. Meditation is becoming a popular remedy to the existential challenges of modern life. In popular media, it is common "to see attractive women in bikinis sitting in the lotus posture appearing to be experiencing a higher state of consciousness." He says that in modern India, the "same glitzy, and often cheesy, new age images of the spiritual life are also abundant" (Cohen 2013).

Cohen still retains a "renewed appreciation for the mysterious and infinite depth that seems to abide just beneath the surface of

India's ever-dusty-and-dilapidated appearances." To illustrate this point, he describes an unexpected encounter he had at Rishikesh. One day, while walking in the market, a sadhu stopped him in the street to spend some time together. Two days later they met at a coffee shop. "As only happens in Mother India, within minutes we were deep in a conversation about the ultimate nature of reality" or nonduality. This implies that the highest experience is the realisation that all of existence — seen and unseen, known and unknown, form and formless, time and timeless — is only one. One happening, one event, one unfolding, in which each of us, is at the centre.

His friend explained to him that he had been writing poetry about his own experience of nonduality, at which point he burst into song. Ecstatically, he sang out loud phrases from his work describing the nature of god. As he did so, the atmosphere between them began to open up in the most profound way. "My heart started to open, as did the doors of perception. I began to experience the palpable presence of the infinite surging between us. The neon lights and plastic décor of our external environment couldn't inhibit the direct experience of the inner spiritual reality that was tangibly emerging between us." Then they spoke about the mystery of the relationship between a guru and the disciple. Since a realised spiritual master is the door to the infinite, he interlocked his thumbs and his forefingers and said, "The relationship with the teacher has to be like this … like one … no distance between whatsoever" (Cohen 2013).

> India's greatest gift to the world still remains what it is most famous for: the gift of spirituality!

The intensity of love that was being shared by them became truly overwhelming. Cohen concludes his article: "Underneath modern India's booming economy and ever-more-commercialised spirituality, the mystery of consciousness, of Brahman, still exists." Then he repeats his very first sentence: "India is still a magical place" (Cohen 2013). Can we recapture this magic and radiate genuine spirituality to the world? That will be the true contribution which India can make to the world.

Science and Religion

30

Science and Religion Must Be Open to Change

We are witnessing a time of unprecedented changes. This trend is most striking in the Catholic Church that is witnessing dramatic changes brought about by the new Pope Francis. His message of tolerance and emphasis on openness to other religions are sowing profound seeds of change. In fact, he has clearly ruffled some feathers among the established order as he encourages the adoption of flexible belief systems, tolerance and compassion. The resistance in some circles notwithstanding, the overall positive wide acceptance of his message demonstrates that change and progress are favoured by many people.

Perhaps, human activities like religion and science have some common elements. Take, for example, Freeman Dyson, a physicist, mathematician and futurist. He says, "Both as a scientist and as a religious person, I am accustomed to living with uncertainty. Science is exciting because it is full of unsolved mysteries, and religion is exciting for the same reason. The greatest unsolved mysteries are the mysteries of our existence as conscious beings in a small corner of a vast universe" (Kafatos 2014).

Uncertainties are intimately linked to change. The constant changes that science undergoes imply unpredictability. Many steps in the progress of science are being built on previous experience and are, therefore, predictable. But some of the paradigm shifts brought by these changes are not. Science progresses by changing the basic assumptions within existing theories of science, claims Thomas Kuhn, author of *Structure of Scientific Revolutions* (Kuhn 1970).

At first glance, many will assume that religions are harder to change than science, since by its very nature, science is constantly open to change. This is generally true. Yet, there are always strong forces in science emphasising the status quo. Those who resist major changes in accepted thinking probably believe they are protecting science from non-scientific abusers. As Kuhn stated, major paradigm shifts in thinking are vital to forward movement. Without it, science, like most human ventures, stagnates (Kafatos 2014).

Today in some important scientific areas, a few scientists are ruffling the feathers of their more orthodox peers. This is, perhaps, most obvious in the field of consciousness, which Dyson declares to be "the greatest mystery of science." Some established dogmas in neuroscience and evolutionary biology attribute the existence and rise of consciousness as "an epiphenomenon ultimately attributing the mystery of conscious awareness to utterly random processes." It is a mechanistic understanding of consciousness.

The unfortunate truth is, "some scientists are more narrow-minded than some of the religious clerics they so easily deride," claims Menas C Kafatos, professor of computational physics, Chapman University, California (Kafatos 2014). When a scientist strays from accepted dogma, not with quackery but imagination, we witness "vicious personal attacks by some of the established keepers of the faith" of science traditions. Kafatos reminds us that science "progresses by debate and solid arguments, not by bullying and abuse." We should seek to protect science from absolutists and fundamentalists. As faithful adherents to good scientific practices, it is our duty to do so.

Science should be open to profound changes in the way we understand nature (quantum mechanics), life (biotechnology) and consciousness (neurological studies). To cling on to stability is doing a disservice both to science and religion.

> "Some scientists are more narrow-minded than some of the religious clerics they so easily deride."

31

Pace of Life Affects Perception of Time

A recent scientific experiment has shown that time indeed lies in the eye of the beholder. It indicated that the perception of time in animals is dependent on their actual pace of life. An international team led by scientists from Trinity College, Dublin, University of Edinburgh and the University of St Andrews, Scotland, showed that the rate at which time is perceived varies across animals. For example, flies have the ability to observe motion on finer timescales than our own eyes can achieve, enabling them to avoid being hit by humans (Trinity College Dublin 2013).

Further, it is interesting that one species of tiger beetle runs faster than its eyes can keep up, essentially becoming blind and requiring it to stop periodically to re-evaluate its prey's position. Even in humans, athletes in various sports have also been shown to quicken their eyes' ability to track moving balls during matches. The study reported in *DailyScience* showed that small-bodied animals like birds with fast metabolic rates get more information in a unit of time (Trinity College Dublin 2013). Thus, they experience time more slowly than large bodied animals like turtles with slow metabolic rates.

Assistant professor at the school of natural sciences at Trinity College, Dublin, Andrew Jackson, elaborates: "Ecology for an organism is all about finding a niche where you can succeed that no one else can occupy. Our results suggest that time perception offers an as yet unstudied dimension along which animals can specialise and there is considerable scope to study this system in detail. We are beginning to understand that there is a whole world of detail out there that only some animals can perceive and it's fascinating to think of how they might perceive the world differently to us."

The lead author Kevin Healy, Trinity College, comments: "Our results lend support to the importance of time perception in animals where the ability to perceive time on very small scales may be the difference between life and death for fast moving organisms such as predators and their prey." This time perception ability can be shown to vary across all animals, using a phenomenon called the 'critical flicker fusion frequency' (Trinity College Dublin 2013). The process, based on the maximum speed of flashes of light an individual can see before the light source is perceived as constant, is the principle behind the illusion of non-flashing TV and cinema screens.

The researchers took advantage of this phenomenon to explain the observed variation in time perception across a broad range of animals, showing that agile animals "possess the most refined ability to see time at high resolutions."

Professor Graeme Ruxton of the University of St. Andrews said: "Having eyes that send updates to the brain at much higher frequencies than our eyes do is of no value if the brain cannot process that information equally quickly. Hence, this work highlights the capabilities of even the smallest animal brains. Flies might not be deep thinkers but they can make good decisions very quickly."

> The world is incredibly more fascinating than we imagine — truly a spiritual experience. We are invited to appreciate nature, ourselves and the creator in a better way.

Luke McNally from the University of Edinburgh adds: "Animals may also use variation in time perception to send covert signals, for example, many species using flashing lights as signals, such as fireflies. Larger and slower predator species may not be able to decode these signals if their visual system isn't fast enough, giving the signallers a secret channel of communication" (Trinity College

Dublin 2013).Technology helps us to watch the beauty and marvel of nature much more closely. The world is incredibly more fascinating than we imagine — truly a spiritual experience. We are invited to appreciate nature, ourselves and the creator in a better way.

32

The Bridge between Science and Religion

Recently, Ian Barbour (1923-2013), a priest and physicist, passed away. Based on his personal experience, "religion provided him with a response to scientific challenge of contemporary world."

Faced with the deadly possibilities of the atomic age, Barbour raised questions that science couldn't answer — a perplexing situation for a young physicist after World War II. He responded to the challenge in an unusual way: after completing a doctorate in physics he enrolled in divinity school and forged a career devoted to bridging the chasm between science and religion.

Barbour was a professor at Carleton College in Northfield, Minnesota, USA, for more than three decades and wrote 16 books, including *Issues in Science and Religion* (1966). This book encouraged the ongoing debate between scientists and religionists on issues such as the origins of the universe, evolution and the ethical implications of technology.

Because of his substantial contribution to science and religion, he was awarded the Templeton prize in 1999 for a lifetime of work that judges said helped to expand the field of theology. In his acceptance speech, Barbour spoke of the need to break down barriers, offering cloning as an example of the ability of science to say what is possible and of religion to reflect on what is desirable.

Barbour's views about the commonalities between religion and science were criticised by prominent scientists, but his advocacy made inroads at such leading organisations as the American Association for the Advancement of Science. He was instrumental in taking questions from the long-standing relationship between science and religion — questions about the origin and future of the universe, the age of the earth, the unfolding of life, or the nature of science — and reframing these in the idiom of modern science and contemporary theology.

> "Religion provided him with a response to scientific challenge of contemporary world."

In fact, he has made significant contributions to interdisciplinary dialogue between science and religion, holds theologian and writer Peter Hess of *The Huffington Post* (Hess 2014). With due caution for reifying such vast areas of human endeavour as science and religion, Barbour identified the principal styles of interaction historically as conflict, independence, dialogue and integration. Methodologically he advocated "critical realism", a view that "preserves the scientist's realistic intent while recognising that models and theories are imaginative human constructs." Barbour was concerned about the danger of absolutising in both science and religion.

This led him to argue that religion — science too — should never be equated with any metaphysical system. "There are dangers if either scientific or religious ideas are distorted to fit a preconceived synthesis that claims to encompass all reality. We must always keep in mind the rich diversity of our experience. We distort it if we cut it up into separate realms or watertight compartments, but we also distort it if we force it into a neat intellectual system. A coherent vision of reality can still allow for the distinctiveness of differing types of experience," he wrote (Hess 2014).

He was one of the pioneers who have tried to bridge the gap between science and religion for the common wellbeing of humanity. He has realised that both science and religion can be liberative or oppressive. So for him human beings need to discern the liberative and humanising potentials in both scientific and religious traditions.

33

Einstein's Thought on Prayer Teaches Us a Lot

"Do scientists pray?" That's the question that occupied the thoughts of a sixth-grade Sunday school class at The Riverside Church, New York. The young girl named Phyllis dared to pose that question to the best scientific minds of her time, Albert Einstein.

She sent a polite and humble note to the great scientist, and she was probably surprised to receive an equally polite reply. This amazing response of Einstein is worth reflecting upon. The exchange was published in the book *Dear Professor Einstein: Albert Einstein's Letters to and from Children*, edited by Alice Calaprice (Einstein and Calaprice 2002).

The letter, dated January 19, 1936, deserves to be read fully: "My dear Dr. Einstein, we have brought up the question: 'Do scientists pray?' in our Sunday school class. It began by asking whether we could believe in both science and religion. We are writing to scientists and other important men to try and have our own question answered." She added, "We will feel greatly honoured if you will answer our question: Do scientists pray, and what do they pray for?" She did not forget to introduce herself: "We are in the sixth grade, Miss Ellis's class." She concluded, "Respectfully yours, Phyllis" (Popova 2013).

Five days later, Einstein replied sharing with her his thoughts on faith and science. The letter was dated January 24, 1936 and Einstein began with the simple address, "Dear Phyllis" and continued. "I will attempt to reply to your question as simply as I can. Here is my answer: Scientists believe that every occurrence, including the affairs of human beings, is due to the laws of nature. Therefore, a scientist cannot be inclined to believe that the course of events can be influenced by prayer, that is, by a supernaturally manifested wish." Einstein was very humble and considerate. So, he added: "However, we must concede that our actual knowledge of these forces is imperfect, so that in the end the belief in the existence of a final, ultimate spirit rests on a kind of faith. Such belief remains widespread even with the current achievements in science" (Einstein and Calaprice 2002).

Then followed the oft-quoted expression of Einstein's religious feelings. "But also, everyone who is seriously involved in the pursuit of science becomes convinced that some spirit is manifest in the laws of the universe, one that is vastly superior to that of man. In this way, the pursuit of science leads to a religious feeling of a special sort, which is surely quite different from the religiosity of someone more naive." The great scientist concluded, "With cordial greetings, Your A Einstein."

> Our spirituality enables us first and foremost to respect each other, learn from other's even contradictory views, and thus widen our horizon of understanding. Spirituality cannot close us to further queries.

While the letter doesn't reveal much about Einstein's own personal views on religion, he brilliantly manages to capture the sublime sense of wonder that science can evoke in a way that it's possible to describe as "religious." He may not have given a direct answer to the young girl's question. But, he has surely given us enough thought on prayer, and the spirit that guides the laws of the universe. Both the believers and non-believers can learn from this exchange of letters how to respect each other and to take one's questions seriously. It is a mistake to regard that we have found conclusive answers, especially regarding ourselves and the universe. Only by posing critical questions humbly and responding to each other respectfully can we grow together as mature human beings, leave alone spiritual persons (Popova 2013).

Our spirituality enables us first and foremost to respect each other, learn from other's even contradictory views, and thus widen our horizon of understanding. Spirituality cannot close us to further queries.

34

When Religion and Science Collaborate

The American Association for the Advancement of Science (AAAS) recently released a large-scale study on the "Religious Understandings of Science," and the findings might surprise many of us. The statistical study, reported in The Huffington Post, on February 19, provides us food for thought.

The survey investigated 10,241 respondents of their views on religion, science and faith. It took interest in the responses from evangelicals and people working in the sciences. Evangelicals are not progressive Christians and generally it is thought that they are opposed to science. So Elaine Howard Ecklund, Rice University professor and lead researcher on the study, was interested to investigate how religion and science can and do coexist in the modern world (AAAS. 2014).

Ecklund had conducted a similar study several years ago in which she surveyed nearly 1,700 natural and social scientists on their views about religion, spirituality and ethics. From her findings, the author noted a surprising trend: There are actually quite a few spiritual scientists in the actual field of scientific research. She says, "Many atheist and agnostic scientists think key mysteries about the world can be best understood spiritually, and some attend houses of worship, completely comfortable with religion as moral training for their children and an alternative form of community." Ecklund refers to this as "secret spirituality." Some said they worried that doing so would cause others to question the validity of their scientific work. The same can happen for religious scientists, Ecklund said, who find themselves practicing a "secret science" in the pews, hesitant to bring up scientific ideas (AAAS. 2014).

> Just like religion is created by God through human beings, science is also God's creation. A true believer can see God through religion as well as through science.

Ecklund's earlier findings, which she outlined in her book *Science vs Religion: What Scientists Really Think*, include: (1) Nearly 50 per cent of scientists identify with a religious label. (2) 14 per cent of scientists have some doubts, but believe in god. (3) 9 per cent of scientists have no doubt of god's existence. (4) 14 per cent of elite scientists are Mainline Protestant. (5) 16 per cent of elite scientists are Jewish. (6) Roughly one-fifth of the atheist scientists the author spoke with say they consider themselves "spiritual atheists."

The newer study on "Religious Understandings of Science" was presented at the annual AAAS conference on February 16 and revealed insights into what Americans think about science. Some of its salient points are (AAAS. 2014): (1) Nearly 50 per cent of evangelicals believe that science and religion can work together and support one another. (2) 72 per cent of evangelical scientists, and 48 per cent of all evangelicals, see opportunities for collaboration between scientific and religious worldviews. (3) Only 20 per cent of the general population think most religious people are hostile to science. (4) 22 per cent of the general population thinks scientists are hostile to religion. It is a positive thing that more and more religious people, including conservatives, think that science and religion can collaborate. Though the general perception persists that science challenges religion and religion will be driven out by science, the actual survey does not seem to indicate this.

We need to affirm that both science and religion are human attempts to arrive at the truth and to make sense of our own existential problems. To the extent they help us, we need to use them for the human betterment. We also need to affirm that just like religion is created by God through human beings, science is also God's creation. A true believer can see God through religion as well as through science.

35

What if We Connect Our Brain and Mind?

Our mind and brain are very closely linked. So, as our mind changes, our brain also changes. In fact, our brain changes both temporarily and permanently. It changes millisecond by millisecond and in lasting ways. As our brain cells change together, they form a common bond. Therefore, Canadian psychologist, Donald Hebb claims, "neurons that fire together, wire together" (cited in Hanson 2014).

Sometimes, the fleeting flow of experiences leaves behind lasting marks on our brain, much like a spring shower leaves little tracks on a hillside, claims Rick Hanson, a neuropsychologist and author of *Buddha's Brain: The Practical Neuroscience of Happiness, Love and Wisdom* (Hanson and Mendius 2009) writing in his regular blog in *Patheos*. Hanson gives an example (Hanson 2014). The fine motor areas of pianists are measurably thicker than those of non-pianists. Similarly, the portions of the hippocampus that are responsible for spatial memory are discernibly thicker in experienced taxi drivers compared with when they started their training. On a darker note, chronic trauma and stress in people lead to a noticeably smaller hippocampus, that plays a central role in registering new experiences into memory. So the mind changes the brain.

Further, Hanson says that the converse is also true. As our brain changes, our mind changes. For example, if millions of your neurons start firing together in relatively slow rhythms — called alpha waves

— we will experience a growing sense of peacefulness and calm. Alternately, if our hypothalamus tells our pituitary and adrenal glands to release epinephrine, cortisol, and other stress hormones, we are inclined to fight or flee. Drawing from the above facts, Hanson hold that we can use our mind to change our brain to benefit ourselves and our neighbours. It may seem a little disorienting at first to think about "using your mind to change your brain to change your mind" (Hanson 2014). But we can truly intervene within our own brain at the organic, material or natural level. For example, consider how we might change our brain with a cup of coffee or tea to feel more focused in a meeting.

Moreover, we can use our mind to change our brain to benefit ourselves in two ways, claims Hanson. First, we can use our mind to activate brain states that promote patience or inner peace or other positive qualities in response to difficulties, such as wounds or tension. Secondly, since "neurons that fire together, wire together" by deliberately cultivating wholesome states of mind over time, we create permanent, structural changes in our brain which may have been there all along. By properly managing the mind, we can cause the "removal of the obscurations" and cause lasting change within ones brain.

These scientific findings of modern psychology and neurology offer incredibly good news. They confirm the ancient teachings of Buddha about the possibility of each person transforming his or her life — even to the point of enlightenment. They nourish our deepest convictions, sometimes called faith: one of the seven factors of enlightenment. And they suggest new practices that may increase the power and penetration of traditional ones (Hanson 2014).

Today's psychology and neurology confirm the ancient teachings of Buddha about the possibility of each person transforming his or her life — even to the point of enlightenment.

In short, today science and psychology is showing the deep connection between our mind and brain. By properly channelising and opening our mind, we can bring about lasting changes in our brain. Thus, we can impact our lives and make them more purposeful, creative, peaceful and adventurous. Maybe time has come for science and religion to contribute to better and deeper human life.

36

Genuine Spirituality Means True Humanity

Every religion promises salvation to its followers. Rarely do we find someone who claims that salvation is experiencing one's own honesty and integrity. Every religion has a mission. No religion understands that ensuring a just and healthy future for whole humans and family of life as its mission. Michael Dowd is a Big History evangelist, evolutionary theologian, and bestselling author, who claims precisely this.

His work has been featured in *The New York Times*, *LA Times*, *Wall Street Journal*, *Washington Post*, *Newsweek*, *Wired*, *Skeptic*, *Discover*, and on *CNN*, *ABC News*, and *Fox News*. His bridge-building 2008 book, *Thank God for Evolution*, was endorsed by six Nobel Prize-winning scientists, noted sceptics, and religious leaders as well.

His basic assumption is that language changes over time and our words create our worlds. He adds: "What we call reality, the ancients called god, or if you lived in a polytheistic culture, the gods. These were personifications of our inner and outer reality." For him, such an insight not only makes sense of religious differences and bridges the science-religion divide, it also clarifies our way into the future.

In his famous TEDx talk titled, "Reality Reconciles Science and Religion," Dowd preaches "the gospel of right relationship to reality." He preaches the gospel of the good news "that is only possible when we, individually and collectively, live in right relationship to what is fundamentally and inescapably real" (Dowd 2014).

He admits that there are many different worldviews that inspire people to live in proper relationship to reality. His passionate path of right relationship to reality, he calls "sacred realism or factual faith." Further, he calls himself "an evidential mystic." He presents the basic tenets of faith succinctly: "Reality is my God and evidence is my scripture. Big History is my creation story and ecology is my theology. Integrity is my salvation and ensuring a just and healthy future, not just for humanity but for the entire body of life, is my mission" (Dowd 2014).

"Reality is my God and evidence is my scripture. Big History is my creation story and ecology is my theology. Integrity is my salvation and ensuring a just and healthy future, not just for humanity but for the entire body of life, is my mission."

His mission for a just and healthy human future calls for "a synthesis of science and religion." It's neither science nor religion but a synthesis that transcends and includes both. As with all bridge-building between perceived enemies, those on the polar ends of the faith and reason divide are less than fully enthused about the "radical middle" position he proposes.

Anti-religious sceptics, he admits, find it infuriating that he lifts up the "evolutionary significance and adaptive value of religion and show how science not only doesn't do away with the concept of the divine but actually offers the one and only way of thinking about God that is undeniably and unavoidably real" (Dowd 2014).

Thus, the many paths that Dowd proposes take us to the beautiful and mysterious depth of the rich and profound reality or existence. The encounter with reality enables us to be deeply human and divine. Such an encounter with the "unavoidably real" God deepens our trust in the reality that is necessarily part of us. Such a deeply religious encounter enables us to go beyond the opposites of science and religion, theists and atheists and even between human and non-humans. The contemporary society needs a deeply personal and collective religious experience that accepts everything, including the good and the bad. Accepting and affirming everything it can wholeheartedly commit itself to a more just, meaningful and viable human future. Thus genuine spirituality begins with true humanity.

37

What We Can Learn from Agnosticism

As an agnostic, the American writer David Breeden is aware that agnostics are often seen as fence-sitters — the tepid ones choosing neither hot nor cold. Why can't they buck up and admit that we're atheists?

Writing in *Patheos*, David Breeden holds that contrary to such general perception, "agnosticism isn't about not deciding. It's about honestly facing what we know about knowing itself." It is, as the Victorian biologist, TH Huxley, who coined the term, said, "not a creed but a method" (Breeden 2014).

Agnosticism is a method like Christian centering prayer or Buddhist meditation. When Huxley first used the word in 1889, he contrasted his confidence in human knowledge with that of the convinced believers. He said, "They were quite sure they had attained a certain "gnosis" — had, more or less successfully, solved the problem of existence; while I was quite sure I had not, and had a pretty strong conviction that the problem was insoluble." So Huxley coined the term 'agnostic,' which is opposed to 'gnostic,' who claims to know so much about life, death and afterlife. Gnostic in Greek means "knowledge." In the west, gnosticism as a movement claimed esoteric knowledge of the workings of the universe. The gnostics claimed to have "solved the problem of existence" (Breeden 2014). Such knowledge, Huxley pointed out, can be neither proven nor disproven. He was not so sure of their untestable opinions.

Gnosticism was not really about knowing, but the claim they make about knowledge or their belief in such claims.

In simple words, according to Huxley, the way of agnosticism "do not pretend conclusions are certain that are not demonstrated or demonstrable." This is not fence-sitting or vacillation. According to Breeden, it is "a commitment to the active search for what we can know. In this way, it is much like the spiritual practice of *via negativa*, a method of removing those things that are not'god' in order to discover god" (Breeden 2014).

Believers can learn from agnostics in asking how certain they are of their own knowledge claims.

However, Huxley saw his method as a positive rather than negative path. So he wrote: "Agnosticism is not properly described as a 'negative' creed, nor indeed as a creed of any kind, except in so far as it expresses absolute faith in the validity of a principle, which is as much ethical as intellectual. This principle may be stated in various ways, but they all amount to this: that it is wrong for a man to say he is certain of the objective truth of a proposition unless he can produce evidence which logically justifies certainty. That is what agnosticism asserts and, in my opinion, is all that is essential to agnosticism" (Breeden 2014).

Huxley made it very clear that scientific materialists don't have the answers either. He affirms that no one really has the answers. All of us find ourselves improvising with as much information as we can scramble together — as have all people for all of human history. Agnostics are committed, however, "to the common human project of learning more and more." This commitment requires them to have active minds engaged in continual searching. Thus the method of agnosticism is a way of being mindful. It is a way of "being in the present moment and making that moment an open and creative matrix."

Believers can learn from agnostics in asking how certain they are of their own knowledge claims. Realising the slippery nature of our knowledge about absolute reality, can we still commit ourselves to the divine? Can we believe in God and still acknowledge that we do not have all the answers? Can we have only one answer — God — and nothing else?

Depth of Life

38

When People Dare to Dream for the World

On August 2012, tens of thousands of people marched to the Martin Luther King Jr. Memorial and down the National Mall, Washington DC, commemorating the 50th anniversary of King's path-breaking speech, "I Have a Dream." They pledged that King's dream includes equality for the poor, the disabled and the underprivileged (Gabbatt 2013).

"I Have a Dream" is a powerful speech delivered by the American activist on August 28, 1963, in which he called for an end to racism in the US. Delivered to over 250,000 civil rights supporters from the steps of the Lincoln Memorial during the March on Washington for Jobs and Freedom, the speech was a defining moment of the American Civil Rights Movement. King declared, "I have a dream that one day this nation will rise up and live out the true meaning of its creed — we hold these truths to be self-evident: that all men are created equal."

He went on, "And when this happens, when we allow freedom to ring, when we let it ring from every village and every hamlet, from every state and every city, we will be able to speed up that day when all of god's children, black men and white men, Jews and Gentiles, Protestants and Catholics, will be able to join hands and sing in the words of the old Negro spiritual: 'Free at last! Free at last! Thank God almighty, we are free at last!'"

> "This is not the time for nostalgic commemoration. Nor is this the time for self-congratulatory celebration. The task is not done. The journey is not complete. We can and we must do more."
> Martin Luther King III

The event was homage to a generation of activists who endured fire hoses, police abuse and indignities to demand equality for African Americans. In the commemoration event, there was a strong theme of unfinished business. "This is not the time for nostalgic commemoration," said Martin Luther King III, the oldest son of the slain civil rights leader. "Nor is this the time for self-congratulatory celebration. The task is not done. The journey is not complete. We can and we must do more" (Gabbatt 2013).

The speech as well as King's personal life was inspired by the Indian way of life. A few years before the speech, on 3 February, 1959, during his visit to India, King told a group of reporters at the airport, "To other countries I may go as a tourist, but to India I come as a pilgrim." Throughout the memorable visit, King recalled, "The people showered upon us the most generous hospitality imaginable... almost every door was open so that our party was able to see some of India's most important social experiments and talk with leaders in and out of government, ranging from prime minister Nehru to village councilmen and VinobaBhave, the sainted leader of the land reform movement" (Gabbatt 2013).

King's trip to India had a profound influence on his understanding of non-violent resistance and his commitment to America's struggle for civil rights. In a radio address made during his final evening in India, King mused: "Since being in India, I am more convinced than ever before that the method of non-violent resistance is the most potent weapon available to oppressed people in their struggle for justice and human dignity. In a real sense, Mahatma Gandhi embodied in his life certain universal principles that are inherent in the moral structure of the universe, and these principles are as inescapable as the law of gravitation."

The dream of King remains incomplete both for the US and for India. Can we collectively dream of a world which respects human beings, acknowledges difference, affirms diversity and fosters freedom? Without respecting each individual for his or her unique dignity and worth, India cannot be the source of moral and spiritual strength — something the world needs so badly today.

39

Do Ecosystems Reside in Our Bodies as Well?

Our belly buttons are a lot like rain forests teeming with life, claims Rob Dunn, a biologist and writer in the department of biology at North Carolina State University, US. His team studied in detail the microbial contents of 60 volunteers' belly buttons, reports Shannon Fischer in *National Geographic News* (Fischer 2014).

The project started about two years ago, where an undergraduate student collected samples of colleague's navel bacteria for a holiday card. Unexpectedly, it was found to be full of various types of microbial organisms.

This gave them the impetus to study our own skin's own thriving ecosystems. "And belly buttons are just ridiculous enough to appeal to almost everyone," Dunn noted. Given the belly button's status as one of "the body's most rarely scrubbed crannies," it offered researchers a chance to study the pristine microbial landscape as close as possible on the modern human.

So in early 2011, the team readied themselves at the *Science Online* science communicators' conference and at the North Carolina museum of natural sciences. The researchers handed out swabs to 60 intrigued volunteers. Back to the lab, the scientists examined the genetic makeup of their bacteria from the swabs. Thus, the Belly Button Biodiversity project had officially begun. From 60 belly buttons, the team found 2,368 bacterial species, 1,458 of which may be new to science. Some of the belly buttons harboured as few as

> "The idea that some aspects of our bodies are like a rain forest — to me it's quite beautiful."

29 species while others as many as 107. The average is around 67 in one person's belly button. 92 per cent of the bacteria types showed up on fewer than 10 per cent of subjects — in fact, most of the time, they appeared in only a single subject (Fischer 2014).

One science writer, for instance, apparently harboured a bacterium that had previously been found only in soil from Japan — where he has never been. Another, individual, who hadn't washed in several years, hosted two species of so-called extremophile bacteria that typically thrive in ice caps and thermal vents.

Even though not a single strain showed up in each subject, eight species were present on more than 70 per cent of the subjects. And whenever these species appeared, they did so in huge numbers. "That makes the belly button a lot like rain forests," Dunn concluded. In any given forest, he explained, the spectrum of flora might vary, but an ecologist can count on a certain few dominant tree types. "The idea that some aspects of our bodies are like a rain forest — to me it's quite beautiful," he exclaimed (Fischer 2014).

But predicting which species might like to call the human body home is only the first step. To make the knowledge useful, scientists need to know why these bacteria show up. Dunn's team is already working on several hundred more navels. They'll use those new samples to start testing the correlation of the navel dwellers with everything from subjects' places of birth to the makeups of their immune systems. Such studies shed light on the ties between our bacterial hosts and their effects on human health.

So, we realise that many species are at physically home in our body, just as we are at home in the universe. In this sense, all living beings are biologically and physically interdependent and interconnected. From this, we can infer that we are all truly connected so that we have a common source and destiny. Cosmologically, we are all one. Therefore, we can truly feel at home in this great and gigantic universe, realising fully well that we ourselves provide home to many. What a marvellous interconnection.

40

Does Good Always Triumph Over Evil?

"Bad is stronger than good" is the title of a scientific article published in 2001 by Roy F Baumeister and three other colleagues. It shows that negative information, experiences, and people affect us much more than positive ones.

The authors meticulously go through topic after topic — personal relationships, learning, memory, self-image, and numerous others — and show that bad has more impact us on than good. They review a couple hundred diverse studies to make this point, and as they say, at the end, the consistency of their findings about the disproportionate impact of bad things (compared with the power of good things) like negative emotions, hostility, abuse, destructive relationships, serious injuries or accidents, and incompetence, among others, is consistent across studies (Sutton 2011).

It examined the effects of everyday good and bad events, as well as personality traits. Undesirable (bad) events had more pervasive effects on subsequent mood than desirable (good) ones. Although each type of event influenced the relevant mood to similar degrees, bad events had an additional effect on the opposite-valence mood that was lacking for good events. In other words, bad events influenced both good and bad moods, whereas good events influenced only good moods.

The same principle is also applicable to personal relationships. Bob Sutton, a management expert in his blog "Work Matters" suggests a way of evaluating relationship. Based on the work of psychologist Dr. John Gottman's "diagnostic index" for evaluating relationships, Sutton reminds us that for a relationship to succeed, positive and good interactions must outnumber the negative and bad ones by at least five to one. Gottman's index suggests that bad events are on average five times as powerful as good ones, at least with regard to close relationships (Sutton 2011).

In everyday life, bad events have stronger and more lasting consequences than comparable good events. Close relationships are more deeply and conclusively affected by destructive actions than by constructive ones, by negative communications than positive ones, and by conflict than harmony. Bad moods and negative emotions have stronger effects than good ones. That suggests that people's desire to get out of a bad mood is stronger than their desire to get into a good one.

That is why bad stereotypes and reputations are easier to acquire and harder to shed than good ones. Bad feedback has stronger impact on us than good feedback. Bad health has a greater effect on happiness than good health; and health itself is more affected by pessimism (the presence or absence of a negative outlook) than optimism (the presence or absence of a positive outlook). Although it may seem pessimistic to conclude that bad is stronger than good, the authors themselves do not think that such pessimism is warranted. In fact, there are several reasons to think that it may be highly adaptive for human beings to respond more strongly to bad than good. So, the authors claim that the greater power of bad may itself be a good thing (Sutton 2011).

"Even though a bad event may have a stronger impact than a comparable good event, many lives can be happy by virtue of having far more good than bad events".

Still, the good can triumph in the end "by force of numbers," claim the authors. "Even though a bad event may have a stronger impact than a comparable good event, many lives can be happy by virtue of having far more good than bad events."

Though the bad may be stronger, it is the basic human tendency to believe and assert that ultimately the good, the true and the beauty triumph. That is faith in the world and in ourselves.

41

Search the Human Heart for Goodness

We try to understand our existence through rational, logical thought most of the times. What is our existence and our life? How do they relate to things and people? How does one event connect to another? What steps do I have to take to achieve a particular objective? Philosophers and theologians ask more fundamental questions such as "Why are we here?" or "What is the meaning of our life?" Another fundamental and life-threatening question is: "Why do we human beings inflict so much of pain to others?" (Hart 2012a).

When one human being kills a dozen others who represent no threat to him, as in the case of a terrorist attack, nothing seems to make sense, and nothing seems reasonable or rational. Such tragedies make us question whether our society is breaking down, whether there is a terribly dark side to human nature beyond the reach of reason and sanity, even whether "the veneer of civilisation has become so thin that it is slipping away," writes Gary Hart, American politician and national security expert, in *The Huffington Post.* Neither politicians nor journalists seem comfortable dealing with these basic issues directly. The same is true of other leaders and ordinary citizens.

According to Hart, we need religious leaders, businesspeople, educators and a large number of people, who trace the causes of unimaginable and unnecessary pain we inflict on fellow humans. We need people who will not ignore the crimes we commit on ourselves, but feel them, reflect on them and suggest creative solutions.

Regarding the terrible harm we do to ourselves, either there are underlying reasons for this about which we can do something or they are so irrational and there is nothing we can do about it. As a human society, we cannot pretend helplessness and let the evil go on. More than the rational analysis of the evil, we need to experience the evil inflicted on us in many terrible forms.

Such unimaginable crimes against fellow humans involve many different factors and have complex relationships. As a student of political theories and systems, Hart says that he will "try to understand irrationality for years to come." But as a student of theology and philosophy, he will "continue to search for a better understanding of the human heart — at its best and at its worst" (Hart 2012a).

Looking at the world around us, Hart is convinced that "there are demons at large that threaten our attempts to understand human existence in rational and spiritual terms" (Hart 2012a). Confronted with the different ways we manipulate and even murder fellow human beings, we need to look into the depth of our own hearts. Searching the dark shades and the monstrous evil tendencies within our heart, we need to focus more on the affirmative, loving and compassionate aspects of our own heart. In this search reason, debate and arguments are helpful, but not sufficient. We need to open ourselves to the emotional aspect of our hearts.

Based on the experience of the suffering of oneself and others, we need to trace its root to our own hearts and come up with radical solutions. Precisely then we need to focus on the common good of humanity; we need to affirm the goodness and rediscover the humanity therein.

Based on the experience of the suffering of oneself and others, we need to trace its root to our own hearts and come up with radical solutions. Precisely then we need to focus on the common good of humanity; we need to affirm the goodness and rediscover the humanity therein. Only by confronting the evil and reaffirming our humanity can we reduce the evil in and around us. Hart is right when he says: "We have a long way to go before we can claim to have rid ourselves of (evil) and to have achieved a truly human society." The first step must start with me.

42

Get to the Depth through Deepities

Our language is limited and so are our experiences. Still we use the limited language to express and to enable experiences.

Deepity is a term employed by Daniel Dennett in his 2009 speech to the American Atheists Institution. The term, actually coined by the teenage daughter of one of his friends, refers to a statement that is apparently profound but actually a triviality.

Dennett defined it thus: "A deepity is a proposition that seems to be profound because it is actually logically ill-formed. It has (at least) two readings and balances precariously between them. On one reading, it is true but trivial. And on another reading, it is false, but would be earth-shattering if true."

Generally, a deepity has two or more meanings: one that is true but trivial, and another that sounds profound, but is in fact false or meaningless. If true, it would be "earth-shattering." So, a deepity is basically the opposite of a profundity and is often used by famous writers like Deepak Chopra. The example Dennett uses to illustrate a deepity is the phrase "love is just a word." On one level, the statement is perfectly true (that is, love is a word). The deeper meaning of the phrase is that love is merely a word without any significance. Such a meaning is obviously false. In fact, love is much more than a word. It implies deep feeling, condition and commitment (Seidensticker 2011).

> We need to admit that however precious our language — and understanding of reality — is, it is limited and open to different levels of interpretations, some of which may be conflicting.

Another example of deepity is: "You learn about nothing from philosophy." The first reading is that the study of philosophy can teach about the concept of nothingness, which is true, but trivial. The second interpretation, which is implicit, is that philosophy is useless. In other words, "You learn nothing by studying philosophy." This second sense would have profound implications if true. Obviously it is not true. So, the statement is a deepity (Seidensticker 2011).

A new age type of deepity may be: "God is the universe" or "God is nature." Sure, we can redefine God to say that God is the universe or nature. Such definitions offer only trivial results (Seidensticker 2011). On the other hand, the profound implication is that we can explain or prove God through the universe is meaningless. A deepity can deceive if the truth of the first (trivial) interpretation is allowed to be confused with the truth the second (more profound) interpretation.

Dennett's contention is that most of the time talking about God or God experience is deepity — trivial or meaningless. Dennett argues that theology is full of deepities, and notes that the sophisticated theological statement, "God is no being at all," is equivalent to "no being at all is god." This can be proved to be a deepity. Other deepities he refers to are: "God is being itself" and "God is the God beyond god." There are many circumstances when religious people take religious language too literally and reduce themselves to trivialities or deepities. But when some people claim to explain the universe and human language through "clear and distinct" analysis, serious problems arise.

We need to admit that however precious our language — and understanding of reality — is, it is limited and open to different levels of interpretations, some of which may be conflicting. Though we all seek the truth, the truths that we possess are partial, paradoxical and sometimes even problematic. This is true not only of our human language, including its idiosyncrasies and oddities. It is also true, as far as we know, of the whole world we live in. Maybe we — theists and atheists — have to admit that such "deepities" invite us to the depth of life and reality.

43

Roots and Routes as our Foundation

Ethnicity and identity linked to both territory and culture. The struggle for ethnicity in the modern and contemporary world is a struggle for plural, economic and cultural regeneration and transformation. Ethnicity as it emerges in between culture and location is linked to our need for roots, said Dr. Ananata Kumar Giri of Madras Institute of Development Studies, Chennai.

He quotes the French philosopher and political activist philosopher Simone Weil: "To be rooted is perhaps the most important and least recognised need of the human soul. It is one of the hardest to define. A human being has roots by virtue of his real, active and natural participation in the life of a community which preserves in living shape certain particular measures of the past and certain particular expectations for the future. This participation is a natural one, in the sense that it is automatically brought about by place, conditions of birth, profession and social surrounding. Every human being needs to have multiple roots."

But our need for roots, many a time, may lead to ethnocentric and exclusionary patriotism. Weil calls this self-idolatry. Today both ethnic and national patriotism in their dominant formation reproduces a logic of self-idolatry, asserts Giri.

However, overcoming this self-idolatry challenges us to realise that there are "routes in all our roots," says Giri. Being with routes does not necessarily produce rootless histories and modernities. Here, our locations are not only bounded locales but are also translocal.

Our locations are "an itinerary rather than a bounded site — a series of encounters and translations," as anthropologist James Clifford tells us. Clifford brings our attention to the fieldwork of anthropologist and novelist Amitava Ghosh in Egypt where fieldwork "is less a matter of localised dwelling and more a series of travel encounters. Everyone is on the move, and has been for centuries, dwelling-on-travel. Moreover, when travel becomes the kind of norm, dwelling demands explanation. Why and with what degree of freedom do people stay at home?"

Understanding the self, ethnicity and nation emerging at the crossroads of roots and routes calls for new modes of engagement and understanding, a border crossing between philosophy and anthropology; both are now deeply parochial disciplines and are still euro-centric in their methods and worldviews. Here, anthropologists not only need to embody deep philosophical reflection, but footwork. As Indian philosopher J. N. Mohanty challenges us, engagement with both footwork and local histories of communities would help us realise how our life-worlds (including ethnic life-worlds) are not only closed within themselves (roots) but are in communication with each other (routes).

> "To be rooted is perhaps the most important and least recognised need of the human soul. It is one of the hardest to define. A human being has roots by virtue of his real, active and natural participation in the life of a community which preserves in living shape certain particular measures of the past and certain particular expectations for the future." (A. K. Giri)

It must be noted that this process of communication is not only a matter of state and social system, but more crucially of actors. For both French sociologist Alain Touraine and German philosopher Jürgen Habermas, such processes call for communicative transformations from all concerned, including the so-called marginalised ethnicities and cultural groups in which creative selves and actors play an important role. They discover their own deep roots and wide routes, affirms Giri.

Thus, as persons and communities, we need roots as our foundation. We also need to experience various routes to arrive at our roots. They complement each other and enable us to be those who realise their own identities and are open to the others.

44

In the Eternal Quest for Reality and Truth

We all know that we live in a three dimensional world. For some time now, serious physicists have been pondering the seemingly absurd possibility that three-dimensional space is merely an illusion. And we may be actually living in a two-dimensional "hologram," writes American science writer David Freeman in *The Huffington Post* (Freeman 2016).

If the hologram hypothesis is true, then like characters on a television show would not know that their seemingly 3D world exists only on a 2D screen, we could be clueless that our 3D space is just an illusion. Then the information about everything in our universe could actually be encoded in tiny packets in two dimensions. "Get close enough to your TV screen and you'll see pixels, small points of data that make a seamless image if you stand back," some scientists say. They think that the universe's information may be contained in the same way and that the natural 'pixel size' of space is roughly 10 trillion times smaller than an atom, a distance that physicists call the Planck scale.

Now scientists at the Fermi National Accelerator Laboratory in Illinois have launched a mind-blowing experiment to show once and for all what sort of universe we live in. "We want to find out whether space-time is a quantum system just like matter is," Dr Craig Hogan, director of Fermilab's centre for particle astrophysics wrote. "If we see something, it will completely change ideas about space we've used for thousands of years." According to quantum theory's uncertainty principle, it is impossible to know both the precise location and the exact velocity of a subatomic particle. If the same uncertainty principle applies to space as well as to matter, space too should have built-in fluctuations known as "quantum jitter" or "holographic noise" (Freeman 2016).

The 21 scientists involved in the experiment will look for the jitter with the help of an exquisitely sensitive device known as a 'holometer'. It produces laser beams 200,000 times brighter than a laser pointer and, with the help of an optical technique known as interferometry, measures jitter in the beams as small as a few billionths of a billionth of a metre. "If we find a noise we can't get rid of, we might be detecting something fundamental about nature — a noise that is intrinsic to space-time," Dr. Aaron Chou, the experiment's lead scientist said. "It's an exciting moment for physics. A positive result will open a whole new avenue of questioning about how space works" (Freeman 2016).

The prospect of making a discovery that would not only defy common sense but also overturn centuries of scientific thinking has Chou thinking in philosophical, almost mystical terms. "I have always believed that if indeed there is a creator, then the mechanism by which the world was created is not necessarily unknowable, and if we delve deeply enough we might reach some very interesting and inescapable conclusions," Chou told *The Huffington Post.* "This topic brings up all sorts of interesting philosophical and theological questions which are perhaps better discussed over a beer or a nice cup of tea. In the meantime, we scientists have a job to do."

> Confronted with the quest for reality — and truth — we must remain speechless, most of the time. The greatness of our little mind lies precisely to pose such questions and come up with some answers, even inconclusive ones.

If the hologram hypothesis is right, then our three-dimensional world is an illusion of another two-dimensional world. The very question on the nature of reality has given philosophical, theological and scientific implications. Confronted with the quest for reality — and truth — we must remain speechless, most of the time. The greatness of our little mind lies precisely to pose such questions and come up with some answers, even inconclusive ones.

Keys to Happiness

45

Meditation for Better Mental Clarity, Focus

The practical usefulness of meditation was demonstrated in a recent experiment conducted by two scholars. They showed that practising a little Zen before class can lead to better grades, according to a new experimental study by Prof Robert Youmans, George Mason University, Virginia, and Jared Ramsburg, a research scholar at the University of Illinois, USA (George Mason University 2013).

The two researchers conducted three classroom experiments at a California university to see if meditation can help students focus better and retain information. A random selection of students followed basic meditation instructions before a lecture. It was found that the students who meditated before the lecture scored better in a quiz that followed than other students who did not meditate. In one experiment, using meditation they even predicted which students would pass and which ones would fail the quiz. The study was published in the journal, Mindfulness, and was reported in *Science Daily* (George Mason University 2013).

The researchers also showed that the effect of meditation was stronger in classes where more new students were enrolled. The researchers concluded that courses meant for new students benefitted more from meditation training than others.

"One difficulty for researchers who study meditation is that the supposed benefits of meditation do not always replicate across different studies or populations, and we have been trying to figure out why. The data from this study suggest that meditation may help students who might have trouble paying attention or focusing. Sadly, freshmen classes probably contain more of these types of students than senior courses, because student populations who have difficulty self-regulating are also more likely to leave the university," explained You-mans, an assistant professor of psychology.

Youmans believes self-reflection might, therefore, have an important place in seminars or institutions with high dropout rates. The study showed significant improvement with only six minutes of written meditation exercise. The researchers believe with more extensive training and coaching, the results could improve.

"Personally, I have found meditation to be helpful for mental clarity, focus and self-discipline," says Ramsburg, lead author of the study and a practising Buddhist. "I think if mindfulness can help mental clarity, focus and self-discipline, then it might be useful in a variety of settings and for a variety of goals" (George Mason University 2013).

> "I think if mindfulness can help mental clarity, focus and self-discipline, then it might be useful in a variety of settings and for a variety of goals."

As an extension of this experiment, Youmans also suggests that, in theory, other forms of active self-reflection such as prayer, taking long walks or even just taking the time to mindfully plan out your day in the morning could have some of the same positive effects as meditation. "Basically, becoming just a little bit more mindful about yourself and your place in the world might have a very important, practical benefit – in this case, doing better in college" (George Mason University 2013).

Such experimental findings that talk about the usefulness of meditation and prayer have to be taken cautiously. Meditation is useful not only for individuals but also for society. But the usefulness of prayer may be explained in terms of the psychological or even sociological phenomena. We need not judge a prayer by its usefulness. Though calming of mind and benefits may be one of the "collateral benefits" of meditation, its real purpose is spiritual. In other words, genuine meditation or prayer is to surrender or abandon oneself to a reality larger than oneself – the divine, God or the ultimate. Surrendering to such a reality has its rewards, which should never be replaced by the practical benefits of prayer.

46

When You Feel a Stroke of Insight

At the age of 37, Dr Jill Bolte Taylor, a Harvard-trained neuroanatomist, had a stroke that traumatised her left hemisphere. Through the eyes of an ever-curious brain scientist, she felt her mind completely deteriorate to the point that she could not walk, talk, read, write, or recall the incidents of her life. Several weeks later, she underwent major brain surgery to remove a golf-ball-sized blood clot that was applying pressure on the language centre in her brain's left hemisphere.

During her eight-year recovery, under her mother's watchful care, she had to relearn most everything — to read, drive and do other chores — because none of her lost memories ever came flooding back. As she slowly got better, she was able to apply her neuroanatomical knowledge toward her reconstituting herself, using her right brain. When Taylor lost the left-hemisphere functioning of her brain, she lost all of the normal abilities to define, organise, and categorise information, but she gained the ability to be intuitive and creative. In the absence of the left mind's describing, judging, organising, and analysing skills, she gained a completely uninhibited right mind, which now processes information in a completely unique way. Her right hemisphere, which typically houses nonverbal and artistic tasks, has taken up the bulk of her knowledge. Taylor achieved her present serenity in an exceptional way and she urges people not to wait for a stroke to cultivate right-brain functions (Taylor 2008a).

So her best-selling book, *My Stroke of Insight: A Brain Scientist's Personal Journey* (Taylor 2008), details the process for recovery and the insights she had gained about the different functions of the left and right halves of her brain. Based upon her personal experience and academic training, Taylor helps to rebuild their brains from trauma. She also educates people with normal brains how they can have healthier relationships with their brains to maximise their quality of life. In an interview with David Kupfer and published in *Spirituality & Health magazine*, she speaks of the techniques to turn off the endless loops sometimes found in the left cognitive mind and turn to the creative right brain.

"I think the most important thing is to consciously choose to bring your mind to the present moment," she says. We decide that we are going to see what our eyes are looking at; we bring our consciousness to the present moment. That implies paying attention to the present moment. It means bringing our eyes and ears to the present moment and start savouring the awareness of the information you perceive. She began as a hard-core western medicine neuroscientist but her stroke made her completely shift from western thinking to eastern experience, particularly to the Buddhist insights. Using the Buddhist ability to experience nirvana, she managed to shut down the left brain chatter. Since her left hemisphere of the brain became quiet, her right side opened up (Taylor 2008a).

Good and bad events will happen to us. But we can react differently to these events. We can say, "Damn, I'm so mad, angry or hurt." Or we can say, "I'm so grateful. I'm going to celebrate those memories. I'm going to celebrate that connection; it is mine forever."

She acknowledges that good and bad events will happen to us. But we can react differently to these events. We can say, "Damn, I'm so mad, angry or hurt." Or we can say, "I'm so grateful. I'm going to celebrate those memories. I'm going to celebrate that connection; it is mine forever." We are called to feel and celebrate what we are as a living being. So, we need to rediscover and cultivate the fascinating and insightful features of the right brain: creativity, spontaneity and effectivity. For too long have we been dictated by the analytical and abstract left brain. But we also need to reaffirm the right brain and rediscover the joy of living — personally and collectively.

47

Dispositional Attitude and Individual Destiny

A new research has indicated the reason why some people seem to dislike everything while others seem to like almost everything. Apparently, it is all part of our individual personality — a dimension that researchers call "dispositional attitude." This personality trait holds clues on the way we react to the world outside.

According to the study, people with a positive dispositional attitude have a strong tendency to like things, whereas people with a negative dispositional attitude have a strong tendency to dislike things, according to research published in the *Journal of Personality and Social Psychology*. The article, "Attitudes without objects: Evidence for a dispositional attitude, its measurement, and its consequences," was authored by Justin Hepler, University of Illinois at Urbana-Champaign, and Dolores Albarracín, PhD, the Martin Fishbein chair of communication and professor of psychology at Penn (Ericson 2013).

"The dispositional attitude construct represents a new perspective in which attitudes are not simply a function of the properties of the stimuli under consideration, but are also a function of the properties of the evaluator," claimed the authors. "(For example), at first glance, it may not seem useful to know someone's feelings about architecture when assessing their feelings about healthcare" (University of Pennsylvania Annenberg School for Communication 2013).

"This surprising and novel discovery expands attitude theory by demonstrating that an attitude is not simply a function of an object's properties, but it is also a function of the properties of the individual who evaluates the object."

However, they note, there is still one critical factor that an individual's attitudes will have in common: the individual who formed the attitudes. To discover whether people differ in the tendency to like or dislike things, Hepler and Albarracín created a scale that requires people to report their attitudes toward a variety of unrelated objects such as architecture, cold showers, politics and football, among others (Ericson 2013). Upon knowing how much people like or dislike these specific things, the responses were then averaged together to calculate their dispositional attitude. This dispositional attitude indicates how much they tend to like or dislike things in general.

Throughout the studies, the researchers found that people with generally positive dispositional attitudes are more open than people with generally negative dispositional attitudes. *Science Daily* reports that in day-to-day practice, this means that people with positive dispositional attitudes may be more open to other people and cultures, do useful things such as getting vaccine shots or following regular activities like recycling and caring for charity, among others.

"This surprising and novel discovery expands attitude theory by demonstrating that an attitude is not simply a function of an object's properties, but it is also a function of the properties of the individual who evaluates the object," concluded Hepler and Albarracín. "Overall, the present research provides clear support for the dispositional attitude as a meaningful construct that has important implications for attitude theory and research." While this theory of "dispositional attitude" helps us to understand the different attitude of people to the same phenomena, the theory also needs to focus on how the individual forms such dispositional attitude. Basically it is the individually, through his or her various life experiences, who shapes the dispositional attitude also. Thus, this theory does not absolve the credit and responsibility of the individual persons.

Still it is a good indicator of how each one of us shapes our own destiny, including our openness to the world and our sense of satisfaction. True, the world gives us different reasons to complain. But still we can be the master of our own selves — though only to limited extents. Precisely therein lies our human greatness and uniqueness!

48

The Mere Pursuit of Happiness Thwarts It

In September 1942, Viktor Frankl, a Jewish psychiatrist and neurologist in Vienna, was arrested and transported to a Nazi concentration camp with his wife and parents. Three years later, when his camp was liberated, most of his family, including his pregnant wife, had died. He was lucky to be alive. In his bestselling 1946 book, *Man's Search for Meaning* (Frankl 2006), which he wrote in nine days about his experiences in the camp, Frankl concluded that the difference between those who had lived and those who had died was one thing: meaning. It was a profound thought which had occurred to him very early in life. When he was a high school student, his science teacher told the class, "Life is nothing more than a combustion process, a process of oxidation." Frankl retorted, "Sir, if this is so, then what can be the meaning of life?"(Esfahani-Smith 2013).

As he experienced from the horrible incident in the concentration camp, those who found meaning even in the most horrendous circumstances were far more resilient to suffering than those who did not. "Everything can be taken from a man but one thing," Frankl wrote, "the last of the human freedoms — to choose one's attitude in any given set of circumstances, to choose one's own way."

He was fond of quoting Friedrich Nietzsche: "He who has found a 'why' to live, can bear almost any 'how'." Frankl elaborates:

"This uniqueness and singleness which distinguishes each individual and gives a meaning to his existence has a bearing on creative work as much as it does on human love. When the impossibility of replacing a person is realised, it allows the responsibility which a man has for his existence and its continuance to appear in all its magnitude. A man who becomes conscious of the responsibility he bears toward a human being who affectionately waits for him, or to an unfinished work, would never be able to throw away his life. He knows the 'why' for his existence, and will be able to bear almost any 'how'."

In 1991, the US Library of Congress and Book-of-the-Month Club listed *Man's Search for Meaning* as one of the 10 most influential books in the US, selling millions of copies. Now, over 20 years later, the book's ethos — its emphasis on meaning, the value of suffering, and responsibility to something greater than the self — seems to be at odds with our culture, which is more interested in the pursuit of individual happiness than in the search for meaning. Frankl wrote, "Again and again, one is commanded and ordered to 'be happy.' But happiness cannot be pursued; it must ensue. One must have a reason to 'be happy'."

> "Everything can be taken from a man but one thing: the last of the human freedoms — to choose one's attitude in any given set of circumstances, to choose one's own way." (Victor Frankl)

According to a well-known editor and writer, Emily Esfahani-Smith, in a recent research, psychological scientists asked nearly 400 Americans aged 18 to 78 whether they thought their lives were meaningful and/or happy. Examining their self-reported attitudes toward meaning, happiness, and other variables like stress levels, spending patterns, and having children, the researchers found that a meaningful life and happy life overlap in certain ways, but are ultimately very different. Leading a happy life was associated with being a "taker" while leading a meaningful life corresponds with being a "giver," holds Esfahani-Smith, in *The Atlantic* (Esfahani-Smith 2013).

"Happiness without meaning characterises a relatively shallow, self-absorbed or even selfish life, in which things go well, needs and desire are easily satisfied, and difficult or taxing entanglements are avoided," holds Esfahani-Smith. Can our spirituality provide us with genuine meaning, enable us to confront suffering and make ourselves collectively worthwhile? Then deeper happiness and joy will follow.

49

In Life, Happiness and Meaning Are Separate

Parents often say, "I just want my children to be happy." It is unusual to hear, "I just want my children's lives to be meaningful," yet that's what most of us seem to want for ourselves. We fear meaninglessness. When we lose a sense of meaning and purpose, we feel sad. "What is this thing we call meaning and why do we need it so badly?" asks Roy F. Baumeister, professor of psychology at Florida State University in Tallahassee, writing in *AEON* magazine.

Baumeister agrees that happiness and meaningfulness frequently overlap. Perhaps, some degree of meaning is a prerequisite for happiness, a necessary but insufficient condition. People may perhaps pursue meaning for the sake of attaining happiness. Baumeister challenges us: "Is there any reason to want meaning for its own sake?" "And if there isn't, why would people ever choose lives that are more meaningful than happy, as they sometimes do?" (Baumeister 2016).

The difference between meaning and happiness was the focus of a study, Baumeister and his colleagues conducted. By interviewing a large number of people between 18 and 78, they were able to see which factors went with happiness and which went with meaning. The following three simple cases — childcare, taker or giver and social ties — make the difference between them clearer (Baumeister 2016).

> "If happiness is about getting what you want, it appears that meaningfulness is about doing things that express yourself."

They asked the subjects how much time they spent taking care of children. For non-parents, childcare contributed nothing to happiness or meaningfulness. Taking care of other people's children is apparently neither very pleasant nor very unpleasant, and it does not contribute to anything meaningful. For parents, on the other hand, caring for children was a substantial source of meaning, though it seemed irrelevant to happiness. This may be because children are sometimes delightful and sometimes stressful and annoying, thus balancing it out.

Again the survey had asked the people to rate themselves as 'givers' or as 'takers.' Regarding oneself as a giving person strongly predicted more meaningfulness and less happiness. The effects for being a taker were weaker, "possibly because people are reluctant to admit that they are takers." Even so, it was fairly clear that "being a taker boosted happiness but reduced meaning."

Then we see that the depth of social ties can also make a difference in how social life contributes to happiness and meaning. "Spending time with friends was linked to higher happiness but it was irrelevant to meaning." Having a few beers with buddies might be a source of pleasure, but on the whole, it appears not to be very important to a meaningful life. "By comparison, spending more time with loved ones was linked to higher meaning and was irrelevant to happiness," holds Baumeister (Baumeister 2016).

The difference, the author argues, is "in the depth of the relationship." Time with friends is often devoted to simple pleasures fostering good feelings while doing little to increase meaning. On the other hand, time with loved ones is not so uniformly pleasant. So the author concludes, "If happiness is about getting what you want, it appears that meaningfulness is about doing things that express yourself." He adds that arguing and debating are associated more with meaning and less with happiness.

Regarding meaning he says that there is no one answer to the question of meaning in life. In fact, there are thousands of different meanings. A life will be meaningful if it attempts to answer questions of purpose, value, efficacy, and self worth. The serious attempts to respond to these questions make our life meaningful.

50

More Does Not Always Mean Something Better

We normally associate the more with the better. The more I have, the better I am. In cricket, the more runs one scores, the better player one is. This is what economists call growth, and we're told that a bigger GDP means we are winning and are on the road to progress. So, the more, the better, the merrier.

Annie Leonard is the narrator of "Story of Stuff," a powerful 20-minute animation movie against the consumerist society. In this film, available for free on the internet, she raises the issue: "What if the goal of our economy wasn't more, but better — better health, better jobs, and a better chance to survive on the planet?" ("Story of Stuff." 2016).

In her syndicated column: "To economists, there's no distinction between money spent on stuff that makes life better and money spent on stuff that makes life worse. GDP treats both the same. If GDP goes up, we're told we're golden — even though it doesn't actually tell us a thing about how we're really doing as a society."

What Leonard calls the "game of more," is accepted by the majority of people as something positive and so desirable. So, she says that we cheer a steadily growing economy, even if the "health indicators are worsening, income inequality is growing, and polar icecaps are melting."

But what if we changed the point of the game? What if the goal of our economy wasn't more, but better — better health, better jobs and a better chance to survive on the planet? Shouldn't that be what winning means? Leonard wants to answer precisely these questions in her new movie, "The Story of Solutions."

Acknowledging that changing the goal of the entire economy — from more to better — is a Herculean task which cannot achieved all at once, she focuses on specific "game-changing solutions." For instance, she wants to contribute concretely towards building an economy that values things like safer, healthier, and fairer "as much as we currently value faster, cheaper, and newer." Such a solution tries to empower people. They value the truth that "happiness and well-being don't come from buying more stuff, but from our health, and our sense of purpose." In the movie, she gives various instances where such solutions are appearing. She cites the case of Evergreen Cooperatives in Cleveland, where worker-owners are running green businesses — a laundry, a solar company, and a super productive urban farm — that are healthy, safe and democratically run.

From a spiritual angle, we need to acknowledge that our well-being and wholeness depend on how we related to each other and now how much we consume — even spiritually.

She also recalls Capannori in Italy, a so-called zero waste town where local citizens, businesses, and government are doing more than "managing waste" better. They are actually challenging the "very inevitability of waste" by working together as a community to find reusable substitutes for disposable products, and put discarded material to good use. In this spirit, she pleads for the "collaborative consumption" (formerly known as sharing). She discerns this new emerging trend is better for the communities. Sharing of cycles, cars and even homes are becoming more common (Leonard 2013).

From a spiritual angle, we need to acknowledge that our well-being and wholeness depend on how we related to each other and now how much we consume — even spiritually. Our traditional spiritual resources remind us that unbridled competition and unchecked consumption are detrimental to human well-being.

Can our spiritual and religious resources help us to change the way we progress both technologically and economically? Can they teach us that living better is far better than having more?

51

Human Bias towards Happiness

There is a universal bias for positive words and happiness in human languages, notes a recent study conducted by University of Vermont and reported in the *ScienceDaily*. The study examined billions of words in different languages, shows that human languages skew toward the use of happy words.

This study confirms the 1969 Pollyanna hypothesis whereby two psychologists at the University of Illinois had proposed the idea that there is a universal human tendency to use positive words more frequently than negative ones. They wrote that, "humans tend to look on (and talk about) the bright side of life." It was a speculation that has provoked debate ever since (University of Vermont 2015).

Recently, a team of scientists have applied a big data approach (using a massive data set of many billions of words, based on actual usage, rather than 'expert' opinion) to confirm the Pollyanna hypothesis.

The researchers found that movie subtitles in Arabic, Twitter feeds in Korean, the famously dark literature of Russia, websites in Chinese, music lyrics in English, and even the war-torn pages of the New York Times all skew toward the use of happy words.

"We looked at 10 languages," says mathematician Peter Dodds who co-led the study, "and in every source we looked at, people use more positive words than negative ones." But doesn't our global torrent of cursing on Twitter, horror movies, and endless media stories on the disasters and tragedies mean this can't be true? This huge study of the "atoms of language — individual words," Dodds says, indicates that language itself — perhaps humanity's greatest technology — has a positive outlook (University of Vermont 2015). Therefore, according to him, "it seems that positive social interaction" is built into its fundamental structure.

To explore in detail this Pollyanna hypothesis, the team of scientists gathered billions of words from around the world using twenty-four types of sources including books, news outlets, social media, websites, television and movie subtitles, and music lyrics. "We collected roughly one hundred billion words written in tweets," claims mathematician Chris Danforth (University of Vermont 2015).

From these sources, the team then identified about ten thousand of the most frequently used words in each of ten languages including English, Spanish, French, German, Russian, Indonesian and Arabic. Later they got the native speakers to rate all these frequently-used words on a nine-point scale from a deeply frowning face to a broadly smiling one. From these native speakers, they gathered five million individual human scores of the words. Averaging these, in English for example, 'laughter' rated 8.50, 'food' 7.44, 'truck' 5.48, 'greed' 3.06 and 'terrorist' 1.30.

A Google web crawl of Spanish-language sites had the highest average word happiness, and a search of Chinese books had the lowest, but the most important finding is that all 24 sources of words that they analysed scored above the neutral score of five on their one-to-nine scale regardless of the language. In every language, neutral words like 'the' scored just where we would expect: in the middle, near five. When the team translated words between languages and then back again, they found that "the estimated emotional content of words is consistent between languages." In all cases, the scientists found "a usage-invariant positivity bias." In other words, by looking at the words people actually use most often, they found that, on the whole, humanity "uses more happy words than sad words," Danforth says.

> There is a universal bias for positive words and happiness in human languages.

52

Christmas Brings the Best in Us

The baby at the manger has become the best symbol of Christmas experience. While one gazes at the that baby a three-fold connection is established. This takes us to the noblest and loftiest of the human race.

First, the baby symbolises the best of the humankind: transparency, innocence and beauty. The transparent child urges us to be truthful, sincere and go beyond the necessary duplicities of day-to-day life. The innocent baby invites us all get in touch with our own deepest self. The beauty radiating from the face of the new born is an invitation to recognise our lost glory and recover our authentic nature.

Besides, the child is the symbol of playfulness, creativity and fun. She exudes a sense of abandonment and joy, which only play can bring about. She also is the poignant symbol not only of the creative act of the parent, but of our own purposeful shaping of life. Precisely in such playful and creative acts, the child experiences fun, frolic and laughter.

Thus, contemplating the child at the simple manger reminds us of the pristine purity of human life. It recalls our common and original vocation towards genuineness and authenticity. It leads us back to our childhood days, when we were true to our own selves, in spite of the normal human weakness. Thus, praying to a child brings out the best in ourselves. It recreates the essential human qualities of hope, vitality and wisdom, which are central to our common living.

Confronted with the mystery that God has taken up on himself the flesh and blood of a helpless human being, we can only fall at our feet in awe, wonder and adoration.

Secondly, the baby at the manger symbolises our natural connectedness to the larger world of parents, pets and planets. Just like the child we too are intimately connected to a few (parents). We are also connected to the larger world of plants and animals (pets). The shepherds tending their sheep were the first one's to hear the message of the new birth. The Bible says: "And there were shepherds living out in the fields nearby, keeping watch over their flocks at night. An angel of the Lord appeared to them, and the glory of the Lord shone around them. The angel said to them, 'Do not be afraid. I bring you good news that will cause great joy for all the people.'"

Further, the three magi of wise men from the east, who followed the star and came to worship the simple child, symbolises our cosmic connection (planets). We draw our energy and strength from our surrounding people, environment and world and are, therefore, grateful for the same. The simple scenario of the manger sends out the powerful message that we live not for our own selves, for the larger world.

Finally, worshipping the baby takes us to the deepest, noblest and loftiest, that is God. Confronted with the mystery that God has taken up on himself the flesh and blood of a helpless human being, we can only fall at our feet in awe, wonder and adoration. At the birth of the child, a great company of the heavenly host appeared with the angel, praising god, saying,"Glory to God in the highest and on earth peace to people of good will." Thus, this defenseless child is god's glory and human's peace. He is truly God in his fullness and human being at his best.

Thus, when we celebrate Christmas, it is an experience of tremendous joy and hope. It reminds us of the best in the human heart, our intimate connection with the rest of the world and our deepest dependence on god, to whom we can fully surrender. It is life-transforming experience of intimacy, innocence and incredulity.

53

So, How Is Your Eudemonia Doing?

A recent scientific study of 9,050 English people with an average age of 65 found that the people with the greatest wellbeing were 30 per cent less likely to die during the average eight and a half year follow-up period than those with the least wellbeing (University College London 2014).

The study was conducted by researchers from University College London, Stony Brook University and Princeton University, US. Using questionnaires, they measured the 'eudemonic wellbeing' of about 10,000 people. 'Eudemonic wellbeing' refers to one's sense of control, feeling that what we do is worthwhile and our sense of purpose in life. People were divided into four categories based on their answers, ranked from highest wellbeing to lowest wellbeing.

Over the next eight and a half years, 9 per cent of people in the highest wellbeing category had died, compared with 29 per cent in the lowest category. Once all the other factors had been taken into account, people with the highest wellbeing were 30 per cent less likely to die over the study period, living on average two years longer than those in the lowest wellbeing group.

"We have previously found that happiness is associated with a lower risk of death," says professor Andrew Steptoe, director of the UCL Institute of Epidemiology and Health Care. He added: "These analyses show that the meaningfulness and sense of purpose that older people have in their lives are also related to survival. We cannot be sure that higher wellbeing necessarily causes lower risk of death, since the relationship may not be causal. But the findings raise the possibility that increasing wellbeing could help to improve physical health. There are several biological mechanisms that may link wellbeing to improved health, for example through hormonal changes or reduced blood pressure.

> "We have previously found that happiness is associated with a lower risk of death. These analyses show that the meaningfulness and sense of purpose that older people have in their lives are also related to survival."

Further, the researchers studied the data on 'evaluative wellbeing.' a measure of life satisfaction, and 'hedonic wellbeing,' related to feelings of happiness, sadness, anger, stress and pain. Various reliable polls show that in high-income English speaking countries, "life satisfaction dips around middle age and rises in older age" (University College London 2014).

"Economic theory can predict a dip in wellbeing among the middle age in high-income," says co-author professor Angus Deaton of Princeton University. He adds: "This is the period at which wage rates typically peak and is the best time to work and earn the most, even at the expense of present well-being, so as to have increased wealth and well-being later in life. What is interesting is that this pattern is not universal. Other regions, like the former Soviet Union, have been affected by the collapse of communism and other systems. Such events have affected the elderly who have lost a system that, however imperfect, gave meaning to their lives, and, in some cases, their pensions and health care" (University College London 2014).

While we grow older, painful and bitter experiences make us more realistic. But some realism could be the sobering realisation that one's life was a failure. It could also be the thoughtful awareness that our life has been worth it, in spite of its failures. The second category will have more emotional and spiritual strength, which will enable them to live longer.

As we grow old, can we get rid of our attachments to failures and success and abandon ourselves to the mystery of life?

54

Warren Buffett's Key to Happiness

Despite being the second richest American, Warren Buffett still lives in the home he purchased for $31,500 in 1958. "Why does someone with more money than the entire economy of many smaller countries choose to live in such a modest dwelling?" asks the social worker Paul C. Milford, in *World of Psychology*.

When asked this very question at a recent shareholder meeting, Buffett responded, "I don't think standard of living equates with cost of living beyond a certain point. Good housing, good health, good food, good transport." Then he added: "There's a point you start getting inverse correlation between wealth and quality of life. My life couldn't be happier. In fact, it'd be worse if I had six or eight houses. So, I have everything I need to have, and I don't need any more because it doesn't make a difference after a point" (Milford 2016).

What Buffett revealed in this response is much more than a guide to financial responsibility. He shared his personal philosophy about happiness, making it clear that happiness doesn't depend on bank accounts. Instead, Buffett implies that after crossing a particular level, the two are inversely related; more wealth actually reduces quality of life. According to Buffett, quality of life hinges upon having good health, housing, food, and transportation. These are fairly basic needs in life. Still most of us search for more things to make us happy. Bigger houses, flashier cars, more lavish meals. The mistake we make is that we try to find happiness in the "ever-fleeting joys of having more" (Milford 2016).

> "The asset I most value, aside from health, is interesting, diverse, and long-standing friends." (Warren Buffett)

Based on Buffett's life insights, Milford makes three suggestions to make our lives happy and worthwhile. First, take an inventory of your life. This is probably the most important thing we can learn from Buffett. Despite having enough money to buy whatever he wants, Buffett views objects as merely hindrances to the true joys in life. "The asset I most value, aside from health, is interesting, diverse, and long-standing friends," he said. The first step to bring your important life assets into perspective is to acknowledge they exist. These are the things we cannot buy. It includes our family, friends, personality, humour, and education.

The second suggestion is to embrace the simple pleasures of life. Buffett once said that a perfect day for him would be to have a whole day of peace and quiet just to read, without interruption. We can take note of the simple pleasures of life and find every opportunity to embrace them. Maybe it is simple things like smelling the roses and making that long due call to a friend.

Milford's third suggestion is to stay true to your core principles and values. Buffett invests in companies in which he believes, rather than in ones that can return the most profit. So he has been quoted as saying, "It's far better to buy a wonderful company at a fair price than a fair company at a wonderful price." This implies that values and principles are central to his heart. Once we recognise our core values and principles and hold on to them gently and firmly, we can make our lives worthwhile and dignified.

By sticking to these steps, we can unlock the key to a much more gratifying life as Warren Buffett does. Buffett's insight is applicable to all of us: "Money will not change how healthy you are or how many people love you" (Milford 2016).

It's precisely the personal health and genuine relationships that make our lives worthwhile and happy. Commitment to values and principles enable us to be happy in spite of setbacks. Conviction and consistency fosters genuineness and integrity.

Suffering and Evil

55

Encounter the Best and the Worst in us

"For last year's words belong to last year's language and next year's words await another voice. And to make an end is to make a beginning," wrote the mystical poet T. S. Eliot. The common celebration of the New Year (2014) presents us with a myriad of complexities, distractions and opportunities. It invites to delve more deeply into our life, to clarify priorities and set clear orientations for the next year.

As the old year draws to a close and a new one begins, Joel and Michelle Levey, founders, *WisdomAtWork.com*, urge to contemplate the patterns of connections and relationship "that weave the various systems in our life together: beginnings and endings, what is developing and what is dissolving." Such contemplation enables us to look into out potentials, strength, creativity, weakness, rigidity and arrogance. Our pleasant and bitter experiences of the past year and the opportunities and fears of the New Year can make of us an "integrated whole."

When any part of our life becomes inelastic, when the flow of energy or information stagnates or when parts of the system become isolated from the whole, then health, vitality and capacity of the "integrated whole" is compromised. From such a perspective, when any living system is suffering from ill-health or impaired in any way, then the remedy is to reconnect it with more of itself and the larger reality.

In the turbulent and rapidly-changing times such as these, we need to seek "to thrive and to discover, affirm and live more fully into our own wholeness." Then we shall be attuned more deeply with our complex, unified wholeness and connectedness to the whole cosmos, with its affirmations and negations.

In this sense of connectedness, the New Year reminds us of our connection with the past and the future. It is also a gentle warning that as human beings, in spite of the cycle of ups and downs, we are truly related with each other and with the whole universe, both animate and inanimate.

In such an organic connectedness or wholeness, we also need to encounter the best and the worst in ourselves and in the world. Realising the ugliness of the evil and the beauty of love, both in our own hearts and in the larger world, we need to resolve ourselves to embrace the whole, accept everything, forgive everyone and move on. Then gradually we shall recognise that "the rhythms of energy and change" within me and around us are deeply related. In each phase of the cycle, we shall be able to see every part of the system in its dynamically-balanced relationship to a larger wholeness.

> "Finish each day and be done with it. You have done what you could; some blunders and absurdities have crept in; forget them as soon as you can. Tomorrow is a new day; you shall begin it serenely and with too high a spirit to be encumbered with your old nonsense." (Ralph Waldo Emerson)

Realising that the same forces that are alive within us are alive and unfolding in the larger world, the New Year awakens us to the mystery of life's circle of birth and death, growing and decaying, becoming old and ever new. Thus, without falling into the "eternal recurrence" so symptomatic of Friedrich Nietzsche, we can celebrate the old, anticipate the future and flow with the change. Then we can remain eternally grateful and hopeful, making our own the prayer of Swedish Dag Hammarskjöld, the former UN secretary-general, and say: "For all that has been — thanks; for all that will be — yes." (cited in Mosser 2011:9)

In this manner, we can be spiritually sensitive to others and be attuned to the insights of the romantic poet, Ralph Waldo Emerson: "Finish each day and be done with it. You have done what you could; some blunders and absurdities have crept in; forget them as soon as you can. Tomorrow is a new day; you shall begin it serenely and with too high a spirit to be encumbered with your old nonsense."

56

To Succeed, Embrace your Vulnerability

Dr Brené Brown's 2010 TEDx talk, "The power of vulnerability," is one of the top 10 most viewed TED talks in the world. She is also the author of *The Gifts of Imperfection* (2010), *I Thought It Was Just Me* (2008) and *Daring Greatly: How the Courage to Be Vulnerable Transforms the Way We Live, Love, Parent, and Lead* (2012) (which the *Fast Company Magazine* named as one of the top 10 business books of 2012).

Brown, a research professor at the University of Houston Graduate College of Social Work, is convinced of the need to embrace our own vulnerability and believes that accepting and affirming our vulnerability is good for the society and individuals. She has spent the past 12 years studying vulnerability, courage, worthiness, and shame. Her ground-breaking research has been featured on various TV shows.

As part of her work she tried first to understand why a handful of people believe in their own worthiness; she calls these people 'wholehearted.' She says: "In fact, I think our capacity for wholeheartedness can never be greater than our willingness to be broken-hearted. It means engaging with the world from a place of vulnerability and worthiness. It implies our ability to be devastate in betrayals and still reaching out to love the others, realising the implied risks."

> "I think if you follow anyone home and you sit at their dinner table and talk to them about their mother who has cancer or their child who is struggling in school and their fears about watching their lives go by, I think we're all the same."

She then lists what wholehearted women have in common. She ended up with two lists: "what they're working towards and what they're trying to let go of." The second list consists of attitudes that are judgmental, perfectionistic, always comparing oneself to other people, ranking everything, very little play, too much work, fear, no vulnerability. The other list had creativity, laughter, joy, play and authenticity. With the help of her therapist, Brown allowed herself to get in touch with her vulnerable side, but it was a slow and painful process, as Helena de Bertodano notes in *The Telegraph*. "It was like a street fight, it was not a glamorous thing, there were very tough moments. I learnt as much about my life from the research participants as anyone else. I didn't come in with this wisdom," she confesses (Bertodano 2012).

Her call to accept our vulnerability and achieve wholeheartedness is applicable to anyone since all of us are deeply vulnerable. "I think if you follow anyone home and you sit at their dinner table and talk to them about their mother who has cancer or their child who is struggling in school and their fears about watching their lives go by, I think we're all the same."

Brown notes that "the difficult thing is that vulnerability is the first thing I look for in you and the last thing I'm willing to show you. In you, it's courage and daring. In me, it's weakness" (Bertodano 2012).

This is where shame comes into play. Vulnerability is about showing up and being seen. It's tough to do that when we're terrified about what people might see or think. When we're fuelled by the fear of what other people think or that gremlin that's constantly whispering "You're not good enough" in our ears, it's tough to show up. We end up hustling for our worthiness rather than standing in it.

When we attach our self-worth to what we produce or earn, being real gets risky and dangerous. The good news is that today people are realising that our titles do not give us success or provide us self-worth. But, do we have the courage to accept our vulnerability and realise the power of our powerlessness?

57

Where Tragedy Meets Eternity

Self-published novel *The Shack* by Canadian author William P. Young, has become a bestseller, having sold more than 18 million copies (Young, Jacobsen, and Cummings. 2007). The title of the book is a metaphor for "the house you build out of your own pain," as Young explained. He added that The Shack "is a metaphor for the places you get stuck, you get hurt, you get damaged...the thing where shame or hurt is centred."

Four years prior to the main events of the story, the hero of the novel, Mack takes three children on a camping trip. Two of his children are playing in a canoe when it flips and almost drowns Mack's son. Mack is able to save his son by rushing to the water, but unintentionally leaves his youngest daughter Missy alone at their campsite. After Mack returns, he sees that Missy is missing. The police are called and the family discovers that Missy has been abducted and murdered. Mack is terribly grieved ("The Shack" 2007).

As the novel begins, Mack receives a note in his mailbox from "Papa," saying that he would like to meet with Mack that coming weekend at the shack. Puzzled by this note, he suspects that it may be from god, whom his wife refers to as "Papa."

Mack goes alone to the shack, unsure of what he will see there. At first, he finds nothing, but as he is leaving, the shack and its surroundings are supernaturally transformed into a lush and inviting scene. He enters the shack and encounters manifestations of god.

The bulk of the book narrates Mack's conversations with God or eternity, as he comes to terms with Missy's death and deepens his relationship with the almighty. God speaks to him about the evil he has experienced: "Evil is a word we use to describe the absence of good, just as we use the word darkness to describe the absence of light or death to describe the absence of life. Both evil and darkness can only be understood in relation to light and good; they do not have any actual existence. I am light and I am good. I am love and there is no darkness in me. Light and good actually exist. So, removing yourself from me will plunge you into darkness. Declaring independence will result in evil because apart from me, you can only draw upon yourself. That is death because you have separated yourself from me: life" ("The Shack." 2007).

"Forgiveness is first for you, the forgiver...to release you from something that will eat you alive; that will destroy your joy and your ability to love fully and openly."

God urges him to forgive always: "Forgiveness is first for you, the forgiver...to release you from something that will eat you alive; that will destroy your joy and your ability to love fully and openly." At the same time, God does not take responsibility for the evil. So, God advises him: "Just because I work incredible good out of unspeakable tragedies doesn't mean I orchestrate the tragedies. Don't ever assume that my using something means that I caused it or that I need it to accomplish my purposes. That will only lead you to false notions about me. Grace doesn't depend on suffering to exist, but where there is suffering, you will find grace in many facets and colours."

Can we relate our intense tragedies to the eternal grace that envelopes us all the time? Can we use tragedies to bring us closer to god? After trying to avoid tragedies and minimising its impact, can we still deal with it meaningfully? Though some people see tragedies and evil as going against god, they can bring us closer to ourselves, others and god. In fact, tragedies can bring the best or the worst from within us. They can drive us towards and away from eternity.

58

Ways of Reaping Larger Rewards

Money is often called the root of all evil, but it may deserve some credit for making us cooperative — at least when we are in big groups. A study of how a monetary system can change behaviour finds that money may have been crucial for the evolution of large human populations. The study found that large groups of people cooperated more when they had a symbolic version of money to exchange with each other.

According to some economists, money has the quality of 'fungibility,' or being exchangeable. Unlike traditional barter systems, where people trade a useful thing for another, the monetary system uses symbolic tokens that can be traded. That opens the possibility of exchanging goods — say, a cow for a year's supply of bread — for which a fair swap would otherwise be too complex to figure out, reports John Bohannon in *Science Mag* (Bohannon 2013).

Beyond its basic utility, money could have other benefits to society. One theory holds that "money makes cooperation possible in large groups of strangers, where trust is in short supply." For this reason, monetary systems may have been crucial for human urbanisation. To test this idea experimentally, a team led by economist Gabriele Camera of Chapman University in California brought 200 people into a room full of computers and asked them to play two different games, both based on the goal of earning points called "units." Everyone started out with eight of these units, and players were divided into groups of two, four, eight, or 32 people, for a series of rounds. In each round, the computer made random pairs within the group (Bohannon 2013).

> "Money makes cooperation possible in large groups of strangers, where trust is in short supply."

In the first game, one of the players in the pair had the option of spending 6 units to help the other get 12 units. That's an expensive choice, but if someone returned the favour in a future round, it would double the investment. Of course, if none gifted 6 units to help out later on, this player would lose. The computer stopped the game after a random number of rounds. Then, the scores were tallied up and converted into hard cash, which the participants took home.

Trust broke down as the group size increased. When just two people played the game, they could count on their gifts being returned when their roles were reversed. And indeed, the pairs of people helped each other out 71 per cent of the time. But in larger groups, the chances of being paired with the same person plummeted — below 5 per cent in the case of groups of 32. The frequency of cooperation in the 32-person groups fell to 28 per cent.

The second experiment was exactly like the first but included a virtual form of money called "tokens." Players had the additional option to use a token to "buy" help from their partner, instead of just receiving assistance as a unilateral gift. Unlike units, tokens had no intrinsic value and could not be redeemed for anything at the end of the game. Still, the participants adopted this monetary system immediately instead of helping each other through gift-giving (Bohannon 2013). With smaller groups, tokens eroded trust and cooperation. But surprisingly, in the large groups, people cooperated nearly twice as often when using the symbolic monetary system, and everyone reaped larger rewards.

Camera theorises that money makes cooperation possible when people cannot rely on reputation or kinship, typical of small groups. He speculates that money drives cultures toward money-based economies by helping to support larger populations. Maybe such symbolic tokens can help us reap larger rewards spiritually as well.

59

Utilise Compassion Instead of Empathy

According to a latest neuroscientific research, compassion may be more effective than empathy. Faced with the intense suffering or distress of others, our natural tendency to empathise can bring us vicarious pain. A better way of approaching distress in other people, according to Adam Hoffman writing in *Greater Good*, suggests that we can cope with others' negative emotions by strengthening our own compassion skills, which the researchers define as "feeling concern for another's suffering and desiring to enhance that individual's welfare" (Hoffman 2012).

Olga Klimecki, a researcher at the Max Planck Institute Germany, affirms, "Empathy is really important for understanding others' emotions very deeply, but there is a downside of empathy when it comes to the suffering of others." He adds, "When we share the suffering of others too much, our negative emotions increase. It carries the danger of an emotional burnout" (Hoffman 2012). The research team sent study participants to a one-day loving-kindness meditation class, which used techniques and methods from eastern contemplative traditions. Participants, who had prior meditation experience, practiced extending feelings of warmth and care toward themselves, a close person, a neutral person, a person in difficulty, and complete strangers, as a way of developing their compassion skills.

> We can "cultivate a compassionate mindset through encouraging cooperation, practicing mindfulness, refraining from placing blame on others, acting against inequality, and being receptive to others' feelings without adopting those feelings as your own."

Both before and after the training, participants were shown videos of people in pain. Following exposure to each video, the researchers measured the subjects' emotional responses through a survey. Their brain activity was also recorded using an fMRI machine, which helped the scientists to see what brain areas were active in response to viewing the videos.

They concluded that the compassion training led participants to experience significantly more positive emotion when viewing the distressing videos. In other words, they seemed better able to cope with distress than they did before the training. The positive emotional approach was accompanied by a change in brain activation pattern. Before the training, participants showed activity in an "empathic" network associated with pain perception and unpleasantness; after the training, activity shifted to a "compassionate" network that has been associated with love and affiliation. Their new brain-activation patterns resembled those of an "expert" who had meditated every day on compassion for more than 35 years, whose brain was scanned by the researchers to provide a point of comparison. This result suggests that the training brought about fundamental changes in the ways their brains processed distressing scenes, strengthening the parts that try to alleviate suffering.

After the training, though the negative emotions did not disappear completely, the participants were less likely to feel distressed themselves. "Compassion is a good antidote," claims Klimecki. "It allows us to connect to others' suffering, without being too distressed" (Hoffman 2012). We can shape our own emotional reactions, and can alter the way we feel and respond to certain situations.

Hoffman suggests that taking a compassion course is not only way to build compassion. Research suggests we can "cultivate a compassionate mindset through encouraging cooperation, practicing mindfulness, refraining from placing blame on others, acting against inequality, and being receptive to others' feelings without adopting those feelings as your own."

If religious people become more compassionate, it will prevent us from the emotional burnout suffered by people in the helping profession. So compassion comes before empathy.

60

Is Virtual Empathy Becoming a Reality?

Are we sophisticated machines? Can artificial intelligence overtake our natural intelligence? More and more often, in different circumstances and for different reasons, this question is raised. This is particularly true in the world of computing and neuroscience. Javier Leach, professor of mathematics at Comillas University, Madrid, is convinced that the answer to that question depends on one's understanding of the real human being and nature. Leach elaborates that a sophisticated machine, which we may call a humanoid robot, may perfectly imitate the thinking and behavior of a real human person. He adds: "possessing the consciousness and responsibility is what characterise us as human beings."

Imitations of human thought and decisions made by machines are improving. This perfection makes many think that soon computers will pass the Turing Test. It is an experiment where a computer tries to trick a human being to believe that it is a real human being, as against a human opponent. The futurist Ray Kurzweil predicts that computers will pass the Turing Test in near future. Does passing this test and showing capabilities considered specifically human make computers truly human?

The newly acquired capabilities of the robots make us question: Is there any difference between the consciousness and empathy that a robot can show and human beings possess? The ability of the robot to perceive human emotions, capturing, for example emotions in facial features and responding with empathy, comes from the perception of human emotions that a robot can imitate and perfect. So Leach asks: Where does the specificity of human consciousness and empathy come from? What does it mean that a robot can imitate human consciousness and empathy? While some philosophers of informatics believe that in the future there will be no difference between human consciousness and the consciousness of a computer, others believe that between humans and robots there are insurmountable differences.

> The ability to perceive human emotions and react with empathy by an advanced computer need not point to identity between human and computer empathy.

However, Leach thinks that the ability to perceive human emotions and react with empathy by an advanced computer need not point to identity between human and computer empathy. Leach explains with a cinematic example. In the film Her, Theodore has separated from his wife and he buys a new operating system (OS) that happens to have a pleasant female voice with an intuitive identity named Samantha. The OS Samantha listens to him, understands and knows him. Theodore falls in love with OS and throughout the film different types of relationships between Theodore, the female virtual reality of Samantha and other female realities are established. But the virtual love that Theodore has with Samantha offers collides with the needs of identity, individuation and personal responsibility for Theodore. To Theodore's question: "Do you talk to someone else while we're talking?" Samantha answers affirmatively. So, Theodore asks further: "Are you talking with someone else right now? And how many?" Samantha answers that she is talking to 8,316 people of OSs.

The answer prompts Theodore to end the virtual relationship. The movie does not give a definitive answers to the mystery of human love and empathy. The broken relationship between Theodore and Samantha indicates that virtual love cannot replace real love and empathy. The end of the film insinuates that Theodore gets a real female relationship. In our attempt to virtualise relationship, love and spirituality, we must realise the preciousness of an innocent smile, children's tears and loving looks.

61

Google's Way to Attain Physical Immortality

It was recently reported that radical life extension is a dream shared by many top Googlers, including Larry Page, the company's CEO. He announced what is, perhaps, his company's most audacious project: a life science startup called Calico that will "pursue solutions for aging and its associated diseases." As *Time Magazine* puts it, "Calico hopes to cure death." It may be remembered that Page actually has a long history with the search for physical immortality, as Ben Popper writes in The Verge.

Page has long been a fan of Ray Kurzweil, the inventor and author who popularised the concept of the singularity, a theoretical tipping point where technology becomes so advanced that it begins to radically alter the fabric of our existence. In the documentary Transcendent Man, Kurzweil openly talks about his ambition "to achieve eternal life, even speculating that it might be possible to bring his dead father back from the grave in the process."

In 2008, Google became one of the corporate backers of the Singularity University, of which Kurzweil is a co-founder. As reported in *The New York Times*, Page and Google provided more than $250,000 in donations to help found the university and several of Google's early employees have personally donated $100,000 or more. In December 2012, Google hired Kurzweil (Dougherty 2014).

The topic of defeating death has become the key point of the Singularity Movement. Last year's Singularity Summit featured speakers like Laura Deming, who said, "There is one fact that never fails to infuriate me. Every day 150,000 die of a disease that we ignore." Deming, a scientific prodigy who at just 18 years, has dedicated her life to ending aging, added, "If we succeed, we will have turned the most awful paradigm that we know on its head. The inevitability of death" (Dougherty 2014).

The study of life science is about genetics, which is becoming a question of computing power and machine learning. "Digital insights are becoming increasingly important in the life sciences, because genetics is a data-driven practice, giving us a real place to add value," says Dr Krishna Yeshwant, a general partner with Google Ventures.

"If we succeed, we will have turned the most awful paradigm that we know on its head. The inevitability of death"

Bill Maris, the managing partner at Google Ventures, told the *Wall Street Journal*, "I'm interested in the ideas that sound a little crazy, such as radical life extension, curing cancer, being able to create a simulation of the human brain and map every neuron." The launch of Calico was met with surprise and excitement. But as Google pushes further in the direction of radical life extension, it would provoke a heated debate. Though we may not be able to achieve physical immortality, the research would bring about other unpredictable possibilities. That a technological giant like Google takes up such issues raises interesting questions. Can we understand and appreciate our lives in terms of technological marvels alone? Can we afford to reduce ourselves to just technological and pragmatic levels?

We need to remember that as human beings, we also need to focus on our aesthetic, moral, spiritual or holistic development. Our humaneness and value systems are intimately linked to social and technological aspects of life. But a one-sided technological growth, without corresponding growth in our human vision and values would be detrimental to our individual and collective destiny. The quantifiable, countable technological growth has to be matched with unquantifiable and priceless value of human life. That is why Einstein had said, "Everything that can be counted does not necessarily count; everything that counts cannot necessarily be counted."

62

Deep Reading Boosts Our Empathetic Ability

Does reading fiction make us better people? Raymond Mar, a psychologist at Canada's York University and Keith Oatley, professor emeritus of cognitive psychology at University of Toronto, reported that people who read fiction appear to be better able to understand people, empathise with them and view the world from different perspectives. Mar later found a similar result in young children: the more stories they had read, the keener their "theory of mind," or mental model of other people's intentions became.

"Deep reading" — as opposed to the often superficial reading we do on the web or newspapers — is slow, immersive reading, rich in sensory details as well as emotional and moral complexity. It is a vigorous exercise of the brain and increases our real-life capacity for empathy.

Recent researches in cognitive science, psychology and neuroscience have demonstrated that deep reading is a distinctive experience, different in kind from the mere decoding of words. Although deep reading does not, strictly speaking, require a conventional book, the built-in limits of the printed page are uniquely conducive to the deep reading experience. A book's lack of hyperlinks, for example, allows us to remain fully immersed in the narrative (Paul 2013).

As author Annie Murphy Paul writing in *Times Ideas* says, such an immersion is supported by the way the brain handles language rich in details, allusion and metaphor by creating a mental representation that draws on the same brain regions that would be active if these scenes were unfolding in real life. The emotional situations and moral dilemmas that are related to literature are also vigorous exercises for the brain, propelling us inside the heads of fictional characters and even, studies suggest, increasing our real-life capacity for empathy.

> Deep readingis slow, immersive reading, rich in sensory details as well as emotional and moral complexity. It is a vigorous exercise of the brain and increases our real-life capacity for empathy.

"Human beings were never born to read," notes Maryanne Wolf, the author of *Proust and the Squid: The Story and Science of the Reading Brain* (Wolf and Stoodley 2007). Unlike the ability to understand and produce spoken language, which under normal circumstances will unfold according to a programme dictated by our genes, the ability to read must be painstakingly acquired by each individual. The "reading circuits" we construct are recruited from structures in the brain that evolved for other purposes. These circuits can be feeble or robust, depending on how often and how vigorously we use them (Paul 2013).

The deep reader, protected from distractions and attuned to the nuances of language, enters a state that psychologist Victor Nell likens to a hypnotic trance. Nell found that when readers are enjoying the experience the most, the pace of their reading actually slows. The combination of fast, fluent decoding of words and slow, unhurried progress on the page gives deep readers time to establish an intimate relationship with the author, who is engaged in an extended and ardent conversation with the reader, like two people falling in love. Literary critic Frank Kermode calls such a deep reading a "spiritual reading" as opposed to "carnal reading" that we ordinarily do. Can we really open ourselves to deep or "spiritual reading," leading to a more empathetic life, where we can appreciate the complexities and nuances of life?

Sadly, deep reading has becomes an endangered practice. Its disappearance would imperil the intellectual and emotional development of generations growing up online. We need to remember that the perpetuation of a critical part of our culture — novels, poems and narratives — can be appreciated only by trained readers whose brains are modified to understand them.

Epilogue

Through these columns which used to appear every week in "Financial Chronicle," I wanted to convey mainly three concerns:

1. Our spiritual life and aspirations are not separate from things that happen to us every day. This implies that if we observe carefully and compassionately at our everyday happenings then the Divine emerges. So, God or the divine is not to be sought in some esoteric experiences, but in the normal events of our life. Thus God is to be found in our life, including in the shadow dimensions of it.

2. It is the experience of God that matters primarily in our spiritual growth. Unfortunately it is generally assumed that God experience is limited to a few mystics, who have the luxury for sustained and disciplined exercise. While not refuting the merits of such sustained activities in experiencing the Divine, I firmly hold that God experience can be found both in the normal sunset as well as in the ordinary flower that struggles to blossom. Such experiences, sometimes even trivial ones, in fact point to the "deeper" or tender aspects of human experience that enriches our lives and makes us more compassionate and loving. Precisely through these experiences, we get in touch with our depth – and our own naiveté – and this is necessary part of our spiritual evolution and growth. Without such depth experience our common destiny is threatened.

3. Science and the secular world have much to offer to our spiritual world. If spirituality has to be lived in this world and God is to be found in the ordinary experiences of life, then contemporary science has much to contribute to our own self-understanding and spiritual growth. Without wanting to absolutise science – or for that matter

religion – we need to maintain a sensitive balance of openness and critique towards the world of science and secularity.

Through these articles I have been trying to communicate such spiritual experiences that enable us to reach out to the others, to perceive the depth in ourselves and thus to embrace the whole reality – including the Divine.

Bibliography

AAAS. 2014. "'Religious Understandings of Science' Study Reveals Surprising Statistics." *The Huffington Post*. February 19. http://www.huffingtonpost.com/2014/02/19/religious-understandings-of-science_n_4811085.html.

Amodeo, John. 2013. *Dancing with Fire: A Mindful Way to Loving Relationships*. Wheaton, Ill.: Quest Books/Theosophical Pub. House.

Association for Psychological Science. 2013. "Brain Can Be Trained in Compassion, Study Shows." May 22. http://www.psychologicalscience.org/index.php/news/releases/compassion-training.html.

Augsburger, Myron. 1989. "The Redeemed Community in a Fallen World:" *30 Good Minutes - Program 3308*. November 19. http://www.30goodminutes.org/index.php/archives/23-member-archives/206-myron-augsburger-program-3308.

Barbour, Ian G. 1966. *Issues in Science and Religion*. Englewood Cliffs, N.J.: Prentice-Hall.

Baumeister, Roy F. 2016. "What is Better – A Happy Life or a Meaningful One? – Roy F. Baumeister | Aeon Essays." *AEON*. Accessed May 10. https://aeon.co/essays/what-is-better-a-happy-life-or-a-meaningful-one.

Beispiel, David. 2014. "Does Poetry Matter?" *The New York Times*, July 21. http://www.nytimes.com/roomfordebate/2014/07/18/does-poetry-matter/poems-hold-the-mysteries-of-the-present-dreams-of-the-future.

Bennett, Jane. 2010. *Vibrant Matter: A Political Ecology of Things*. Durham: Duke University Press.

Bertodano, Helena de. 2012. "Brené Brown on the Power of Vulnerability." *The Telegraph*. September 17. http://www.telegraph.co.uk/women/sex/self-help/9536381/Brene-Brown-on-the-power-of-vulnerability.html.

Bohannon, John. 2013. "Does Money Inspire Us to Cooperate?" *Science | AAAS*. August 26. http://www.sciencemag.org/news/2013/08/does-money-inspire-us-cooperate.

Breeden, David. 2014. "The Spiritual Practice of Agnosticism." *Patheos*. August 28. http://www.patheos.com/blogs/uucollective/2014/08/the-spiritual-practice-of-agnosticism/?webSyncID=7bc5c65a-b934-dd81-cc4e-337dd2912413&sessionGUID=09e40b6c-5c24-4ce0-ec11-61ea17432dc9.

Brown, Brené. 2008. *I Thought it Was Just Me (but it Isn't): Telling the Truth about Perfectionism, Inadequacy, and Power*. New York: Gotham Books.

Brown, Brené. 2010. *The Gifts of Imperfection: Let Go of who You Think You're Supposed to Be and Embrace who You Are*. Center City, Minnesota: Hazelden Foundation.

Brown, Brené. 2012. *Daring Greatly: How the Courage to Be Vulnerable Transforms the Way We Live, Love, Parent, and Lead*. New York, NY: Gotham Books.

Campbell, Polly L. 2012. *Imperfect Spirituality: Extraordinary Enlightenment for Ordinary People*. Berkeley, California: Viva Editions.

Chomsky, Noam. 2014. "How Many Minutes to Midnight?" *The Huffington Post*. October 5. http://www.huffingtonpost.com/entry/hiroshima-day-2014_b_5650658.html?section=india.

Cohen, Andrew. 2013. "India's True Prosperity." *Big Think*. March 25. http://bigthink.com/the-evolution-of-enlightenment/indias-true-prosperity.

Dougherty, Conor. 2014. "Calico, Google's Anti-Aging Company, Announces New Research Facility" *The New York Times*. September 3. http://bits.blogs.nytimes.com/2014/09/03/googles-anti-aging-company-announces-new-research-facility/?_r=0.

Dowd, Miachael. 2014. "Rebooting Religion for Climate Action." *Pastordawn*. September 10. https://pastordawn.com/tag/michael-dowd/.

Dowd, Michael. 2008. *Thank God for Evolution: How the Marriage of Science and Religion will Transform Your Life and Our World.* New York: Viking.

Einstein, Albert, and Alice Calaprice. 2002. *Dear Professor Einstein: Albert Einstein's Letters to and from Children*. Amherst, N.Y.: Prometheus Books.

Elgin, Duane. 1993. *Voluntary Simplicity : Toward a Way of Life that is Outwardly Simple, Inwardly Rich*. New York: Quill.

Elgin, Duane. 2011. "Progress Can Make Us More Spiritual, Not Less." *The Huffington Post*. November 13. http://www.huffingtonpost.com/entry/progress-and-simplicity_b_957446.html?section=india.

Emory Health Sciences. (2014, January 3). A novel look at how stories may change the brain. *Science Daily*. Retrieved May 9, 2016 from www.sciencedaily.com/releases/2014/01/140103204428.htm.

Ericson, John. 2013. "A Scientific Theory of Haters." *Medical Daily*. August 26. http://www.medicaldaily.com/scientific-theory-haters-dispositional-attitudes-determine-negative-and-positive-responses-new-study.

Esfahani-Smith, Emily. 2013. "There's more to Life than Being Happy." *The Atlantic*. January 9. http://www.theatlantic.com/health/archive/2013/01/theres-more-to-life-than-being-happy/266805/.

Fischer, Shannon. 2014. "What Lives in Your Belly Button? Study Finds 'Rain Forest' of Species." November 14. http://news.nationalgeographic.com/news/2012/11/121114-belly-button-bacteria-science-health-dunn/.

Frankl, Viktor E. 2006. *Man's Search for Meaning*. Boston: Beacon Press.

Freeman, David. 2016. "Top Scientists Weigh in on Whether We All Live in a Hologram." *The Huffington Post.* April 7. http://www.huffingtonpost.com/entry/universe-simulation-live-debate_us_5703d091e4b0a06d5806e344?section=india.

Gabbatt, Adam. 2013. "March on Washington: Thousands Arrive for 50th Anniversary – as It Happened." *The Guardian.* August 24. http://www.theguardian.com/world/2013/aug/24/march-on-washington-martin-luther-king-50-years.

George Mason University. (2013, April 9). Meditating before lecture leads to better grades. *Science Daily.* Retrieved May 9, 2016 from www.sciencedaily.com/releases/2013/04/130409131811.htm.

Goldstein, Elisha. 2012. *The Now Effect: How this Moment Can Change the Rest of Your Life.* New York: Atria Books.

Goldstein, Elisha. 2013. "Top 5 Regrets of the Dying." *The Huffington Post.* November 11. http://www.huffingtonpost.com/entry/life-lessons_b_3862875.html?section=india.

Guessoum, Nidhal. 2013. "Why Should Scientists Care About Religion?" *BQO.* August 19. https://www.bigquestionsonline.com/2013/08/19/why-should-scientists-care-about-religion/.

Hanson, Bradley. 2014. *Spirituality and Your Life Story.* Bloomington, IN: Archway Publishing.

Hanson, Rick, and Richard Mendius. 2009. *Buddha's Brain the Practical Neuroscience of Happiness, Love, & Wisdom.* Oakland, CA: New Harbinger Publications.

Hanson, Rick. 2014. "Mind Changing Brain Changing Mind." *Patheos: Just One Thing.* January 24. http://www.patheos.com/blogs/justonething/2014/01/mind-changing-brain-changing-mind/.

Harmon, A. G. 2014. "Lessons of the Giver." *Patheos.* August 26. http://www.patheos.com/blogs/goodletters/2014/08/lessons-of-the-giver/.

Hart, Gary. 2012. "Amusing Ourselves to Death." *Matters of Principle.* June 22. http://www.mattersofprinciple.com/?p=912.

Hart, Gary. 2012a. "The Search for Humanity Continues." *The Huffington Post*. September 20. http://www.huffingtonpost.com/entry/aurora-shooting_b_1691705.html?section=india.

Herbert, Wray. 2010. *On Second Thought: Outsmarting Your Mind's Hard-Wired Habits*. New York: Crown Publishers.

Hess, Peter. 2014. "An Appreciation of Ian G. Barbour (1923-2013)." *The Huffington Post*. March 11. http://www.huffingtonpost.com/peter-m-j-hess-phd/ian-g-barbour_b_4557453.html.

Hoffman, Adam. 2012. "When Empathy Hurts, Compassion Can Heal | Greater Good." *Greater Good*. August 22. http://greatergood.berkeley.edu/article/item/when_empathy_hurts_compassion_can_heal.

Jaber, Ferris. 2014. "Why Nothing Is Truly Alive." *The New York Times*. March 12. http://www.nytimes.com/2014/03/13/opinion/why-nothing-is-truly-alive.html?_r=0.

James, William. 1936. *The Varieties of Religious Experience: A Study in Human Nature*.

Jenkins, Jessica Kerwin. 2010. *Encyclopedia of the Exquisite: An Anecdotal History of Elegant Delights*. New York: Nan A. Talese/Doubleday.

Jenkins, Jessica Kerwin. 2013. "Homage to the Idols of Idleness." *The New York Times*. November 29. http://www.nytimes.com/2013/11/30/opinion/homage-to-the-idols-of-idleness.html.

Jenkins, Jessica Kerwin. 2013a. *All the Time in the World: A Book of Hours*.

Kafatos, Menas C. 2014. "Religion Is Changing, So Why Not Science?" *The Huffington Post*. February 19. http://www.huffingtonpost.com/menas-c-kafatos/religion-is-changing-so-why-not-science_b_4457621.html.

Kasser, Tim. 2002. *The High Price of Materialism*. Cambridge, Massachusetts: MIT Press.

Kuhn, Thomas S. 1970. *The Structure of Scientific Revolutions.* Chicago: University of Chicago Press.

Leonard, Annie. 2013. "The Story of Solutions: Better, Not More - Our World." October 11. http://ourworld.unu.edu/en/the-story-of-solutions.

Lilienfeld, S. O, and R. Ammirati. 2014. "Would the World Be Better Off Without Religion? A Skeptic's Guide to the Debate." *SKEPTICAL INQUIRER* 38 (4): 30.

Lilienfeld, S. O, and R. Ammirati. 2014. "Would the World Be Better Off Without Religion? A Skeptic's Guide to the Debate." *SKEPTICAL INQUIRER* 38 (4): 30.

Lonergan, Bernard J. F, 1992. *Insight a Study of Human Understanding.* Toronto; Buffalo: Published for Lonergan Research Institute of Regis College, Toronto, by University of Toronto Press.

Lowry, Lois. 2014. *The Giver.* London: HarperCollins.

Luhrmann, T. M. 2014. "Where Reason Ends and Faith Begins - The New York Times." July 26. http://www.nytimes.com/2014/07/27/opinion/sunday/t-m-luhrmann-where-reason-ends-and-faith-begins.html?_r=0.

Lurie, Alan J. 2009. *Five Minutes on Mondays: Finding Unexpected Purpose, Peace, and Fulfillment at Work.* Upper Saddle River, N.J.: FT Press.

Lurie, Alan J. 2011. "The Allure of Narcissistic Spirituality." *The Huffington Post.* November 27. http://www.huffingtonpost.com/entry/the-allure-of-spiritual-n_b_803415.html?section=india.

Mehta, Pavithra. 2014. "Giftivism: Reclaiming the Priceless." *DailyGood.* January 15. http://www.dailygood.org/story/644/giftivism-reclaiming-the-priceless-pavithra-mehta/.

Milford, Paul C. 2016. "How Warren Buffett Found the Key to Happiness." *World of Psychology: Psych Central.com.* Accessed May 10. http://psychcentral.com/blog/archives/2014/08/08/how-warren-buffett-found-the-key-to-happiness/.

Mosser, David. 2011. *Transitions: Leading Churches through Change.* Louisville, Kentucky: Westminster John Knox Press.

Paul, Annie Murphy. 2013. "Reading Literature Makes Us Smarter and Nicer." *Time.com.* June 3. http://ideas.time.com/2013/06/03/why-we-should-read-literature/.

Piketty, Thomas. 2014. *Capital in the Twenty-First Century.* Cambridge, Massachusetts: The Belknap Press of Harvard University Press. http://www.worldcat.org/title/capital-in-the-twenty-first-century/oclc/858914389&referer=brief_results.

Popova, Maria. 2013. "Do Scientists Pray? Einstein Answers a Little Girl's Question about Science vs. Religion." *Brain Pickings.* July 11. https://www.brainpickings.org/2013/07/11/do-scientists-pray-einstein-letter-science-religion/.

Popova, Maria. 2014. "Wisdom in the Age of Information and the Importance of Storytelling in Making Sense of the World: An Animated Essay." *Brain Pickings.* September 9. https://www.brainpickings.org/2014/09/09/wisdom-in-the-age-of-information/.

Postman, Neil. 1985. *Amusing Ourselves to Death: Public Discourse in the Age of Show Business.* New York: Viking.

Rahman, Maseeh. 2013. "Indian Anti-Superstition Activist Narendra Dabholkar Shot Dead." *The Guardian.* August 20. http://www.theguardian.com/world/2013/aug/20/anti-superstition-narendra-dabholkar-shot-dead.

Seidensticker, Bob. 2011. "Word of the Day: Deepity." *Patheos.* November 5. http://www.patheos.com/blogs/crossexamined/2011/11/word-of-the-day-deepity/.

Shenoy, Suchitra, and Pavithra Mehta. 2011. *Infinite Vision.* Berrett-Koehler Publishers. http://www.myilibrary.com?id=329345.

Simms, Andrew, and Ruth Potts. 2012. *The New Materialism: How Our Relationship with the Material World Can Change for the Better.* London: The Real Press.

Stevenson, Robert Louis. 1905. *An Apology for Idlers and Other Essays.* Portland, Maine: Thomas Bird Mosher.

"'Spirituality and Your Life Story.'" 2014. June 20. http://www.decorahnewspapers.com/Content/Social/Social/Article/-Spirituality-and-Your-Life-Story--/-2/-2/34765.

"Story of Stuff." 2016. Accessed May 10. http://storyofstuff.org/.

Sutton, Bob. 2011. "Bad is Stronger than Good: Why Eliminating the Negative is More Important than Accentuating the Positive." *Work Matters*. October 24. http://bobsutton.typepad.com/my_weblog/2011/10/bad-is-stronger-than-good-why-eliminating-the-negative-is-more-important-than-accentuating-the-posit.html.

Tartakovsky, Margarita. 2016. "3 Ways to Develop a Spiritual Practice | World of Psychology." *World of Psychology*. Accessed May 9. http://psychcentral.com/blog/archives/2014/06/19/3-ways-to-develop-a-spiritual-practice/.

Taylor, Jill Bolte. 2008. *My Stroke of Insight: A Brain Scientist's Personal Journey*. New York: Viking.

Taylor, Jill Bolte. 2008a. "Transcript of 'My Stroke of Insight.'" https://www.ted.com/talks/jill_bolte_taylor_s_powerful_stroke_of_insight/transcript.

Thoreau, Henry David. 1962. *Walden*. New York: Time Inc.

"The Shack." 2007. *Goodreads*. July 1. http://www.goodreads.com/work/best_book/2666268-the-shack-where-tragedy-confronts-eternity.

Thorpe, Nick. 2016. "The New Materialism." *AEON*. Accessed May 9. http://www.nickthorpe.co.uk/new-materialism/.

Toynbee, Arnold, and D. C. Somervell. 1947. *A Study of History*. New York: Oxford University Press.

Trinity College Dublin. (2013, September 16). Time is in the eye of the beholder: Time perception in animals depends on their pace of life. *ScienceDaily*. Retrieved May 9, 2016 from www.sciencedaily.com/releases/2013/09/130916102006.htm.

Tucker, Evelyn, and Brian Swimme. 2016. "To Be Human." *Center for Humans & Nature*. Accessed May 11. http://www.

humansandnature.org/to-be-human-mary-evelyn-tucker-brian-swimme.

University College London. (2014, November 6). Sense of meaning and purpose in life linked to longer lifespan. *ScienceDaily*. Retrieved May 11, 2016 from www.sciencedaily.com/releases/2014/11/141106211618.htm.

University of Pennsylvania Annenberg School for Communication. (2013, August 26). Why do haters have to hate? Newly identified personality trait holds clues. *ScienceDaily*. Retrieved May 9, 2016 from www.sciencedaily.com/releases/2013/08/130826123147.htm.

University of St Andrews. 2014. "Forgive to Forget." May 13. https://www.st-andrews.ac.uk/news/archive/2014/title,242493,en.php.

University of Vermont. (2015, February 9). F-bombs notwithstanding, all languages skew toward happiness: Universal human bias for positive words. *Science Daily*. Retrieved May 11, 2016 from www.sciencedaily.com/releases/2015/02/150209161143.htm.

Ware, Bronnie. 2012. *The Top Five Regrets of the Dying: A Life Transformed by the Dearly Departing*. Carlsbad, California: Hay House.

Widrich, Leo. 2012. "The Science of Storytelling: Why Telling a Story is the Most Powerful Way to Activate Our Brains." *Lifehacker*. December 5. http://lifehacker.com/5965703/the-science-of-storytelling-why-telling-a-story-is-the-most-powerful-way-to-activate-our-brains.

Wilde, Oscar. 1998. *Oscar Wilde's Wit and Wisdom: A Book of Quotations*. Mineola, N.Y.: Dover Publications.

Wolf, Maryanne, and Catherine J. Stoodley. 2007. *Proust and the Squid: The Story and Science of the Reading Brain*. New York, NY: Harper.

Young, William P., Wayne Jacobsen, and Brad Cummings. 2007. *The Shack: Where Tragedy Confronts Eternity*. Newbury Park, California: Windblown Media.

Index